Contesting Apartheid

Contesting Apartheid

U.S. Activism, 1960–1987

Donald R. Culverson

Westview Press

A Member of the Perseus Books Group

Copyright © 1999 by Westview Press, A Member of the Perseus Books Group

Published in 1999 in the United States of America by Westview Press, 5500 Central Avenue, Boulder, Colorado 80301-2877, and in the United Kingdom by Westview Press, 12 Hid's Copse Road, Cumnor Hill, Oxford OX2 9JJ

Library of Congress Cataloging-in-Publication Data
Culverson, Donald R.
    Contesting apartheid : U.S. activism, 1960–1987 / Donald R. Culverson.
        p.   cm.
    Includes bibliographical references (p.   ) and index.
    ISBN 0-8133-6669-0
    1. United States—Relations—South Africa.   2. South Africa—Relations—United States.   3. Anti-apartheid movements—United States—History.   I. Title.
E183.8.S6C85   1999
327.73068'09'045—dc21   99-22528
                                                                                          CIP

The paper used in this publication meets the requirements of the American National Standard for Permanence of Paper for Printed Library Materials Z39.48-1984.

10   9   8   7   6   5   4   3   2   1

Contents

Tables and Illustrations

Contesting Apartheid

Introduction

From 1984 to 1986, the Free South Africa Movement (FSAM), a coalition of anti-apartheid groups, sustained a grassroots mobilization against U.S. relations with South Africa that prompted local and state governments, corporations, banks, churches, and academic institutions to reassess their ties to the apartheid system. This activism, combined with increased international efforts to isolate South Africa and intensifying internal opposition to the regime, led Congress to pass a package of limited sanctions in November 1986. The Anti-Apartheid Act revealed that concern about racial injustice in South Africa had deeply penetrated American politics. It increased the number of venues where both proponents and opponents of disengagement could debate, captured media attention, attracted politicians and celebrities, and removed evasion as an option for many national public and private institutions.

The visibility and salience of the FSAM generated a range of scholarly interpretations. Although some observers viewed the movement's growth as evidence of the continuing viability of pluralist strategies for previously marginalized groups,[1] others contended that the FSAM's reliance on media representations of this popular movement produced only symbolic gains. Other accounts described anti-apartheid strategies and tactics as organic extensions of the post–World War II civil rights movement.[2] Although all of these interpretations capture aspects of anti-apartheid dynamics, they obscure the movement's scope and depth by confining it to a particular context and temporal frame, thus masking nearly a century of American opposition to racial oppression in South Africa.

The study of anti-apartheid activism is significant because it illuminates both familiar and novel challenges to political participation patterns in American society. Opponents of U.S. government and corporate relations with South Africa attempted not only to democratize policy processes traditionally dominated by elite institutions but also to use the collective memory of America's racial experiences as a catalyst for challenging these power inequalities. In so doing, however, they were ahead of the game. Some literature depicts anti-apartheid activists as relying upon the symbols, strategies, resources, and access supplied by the domestic civil rights movement.[3] Activists drew analogies between the United States and South Africa and exposed persistent racial anachronisms in the construction of American relations with that republic and the other white settler states. The complementarities between racial issues in the two countries may have proved useful instruments for antiracist struggle in both nations, but history reveals that many of the characteristics of popular anti-apartheid activism in the United States predate such civil rights milestones as the Montgomery bus boycott.[4]

Examination of grassroots mobilization against apartheid also reveals alterations in the material and ideational base that engender contemporary social and political movements. Structural transformations in advanced capitalist societies presented activists with new arrangements of resources, technologies, audiences, and obstacles. These changes provided popular movements with potent information on the degree of U.S. institutional involvement and on interdependence within a global system.

Developing a more thorough understanding of anti-apartheid activism requires challenging conventional categorizations and constructions. Disciplinary and subfield barriers that restrict the study of anti-apartheid mobilization to the margins of academic inquiry must be contested. This book examines how, since 1960, U.S. citizen groups have been drawn to the issue, not just to challenge government and corporate policy but also to develop more comprehensive explanations of American connections to the production and distribution of wealth and poverty in southern Africa and to expand options for transnational citizen activism.

Three major objectives motivate this study. The first is the need to apply the critical analysis developed in studying social movements to the study of anti-apartheid mobilization. The second goal is to examine how political science deals with social movements, particularly those that operate beyond national boundaries and thus challenge traditional conceptions of the nature and practice of politics. The third objective is to address some general propositions that emerge from the existing literature on social movements, studies of transnational activism, and new data sources on key organizations.

Throughout nearly three centuries of American contact with South Africa, Americans have acted on their concerns about the system of racial dominance and exploitation. *Contesting Apartheid* asserts that anti-apartheid activism represents a rational effort to promote change and restrain further American complicity with the systematic erosion of human rights in South Africa. It also affirms that anti-apartheid struggle occurred more frequently than conventional wisdom suggests and that protest activities cut across race and class lines.

The circumstances that enable social movement activity reflect the values of established institutions that tend to outline fundamental aspects of politics: what constitutes politics, who can participate politically, what the rewards and punishments of participation are, and the boundaries of politics. Representations of the national interest, ideas about appropriate race relations, and the structures of national and state governments have enormously influenced the ability of activists to mobilize constituencies against apartheid. Not surprisingly, then, opportunities available to citizens to protest objectionable foreign policy decisions differ from those associated with domestic political participation.

Whereas conventional groups concerned with exerting influence on domestic policies concentrate their energies on gaining access to identifiable points in the policymaking process, popular transnational efforts must not only negotiate a maze of governmental units engaged in foreign affairs but also contest the cultural and often legal prohibitions on extending participatory practices beyond established barriers. Until recently, scholars narrowly perceived such endeavors as expressive of identity politics or as symbolically oriented rather than as indicative of legitimate claims to political influence and power. The increasing sophistication of social movement theory and growing scholarly interest in the processes of global interaction make anti-apartheid activism a timely subject.[5]

Chapter 1 presents an overview of recent developments in social movement theory. It outlines political process theory and briefly compares it to classical, resource mobilization, and new social movement approaches. Chapter 2 examines how the structure of South African–American relations from the late nineteenth century through the early the Cold War years routinely excluded anti-apartheid concerns from debate. When presenting the problem of South African racism to federal officials, American missionaries and civil rights activists attempted to politicize grievances, but humanitarian concerns could not infringe upon the terrain occupied by the dominant economic and political interests that shaped U.S. policy. Chapter 3 investigates the emergence of American anti-apartheid activism in the aftermath of the 1960 Sharpeville massacre. It focuses on the domestic and international climates that framed how American public and private sector institutions—whether opponents or supporters of apartheid—reacted to Sharpeville. It traces how those responses altered grassroots mobilization efforts throughout the 1960s. Chapter 4 explores the process by which the anti-apartheid movement gained structural access during the 1970s. This included the establishment of profitable linkages with grassroots organizations, social-conscience constituencies, and congressional subcommittees; the weakening of the national consensus on foreign policy; and the collapse of Portugal's empire in southern Africa. Chapter 5 analyzes how deepening U.S. entanglements in southern Africa enabled racial inequality to penetrate American politics in ways that invited comparisons to domestic struggles over civil rights and the Vietnam War. Chapter 6 traces the path of anti-apartheid activism from the mid-seventies to the early eighties. It demonstrates that reduction in structural access did not present an insurmountable barrier to mobilization efforts. Chapter 7 explores the convergence of forces that enabled anti-apartheid organizations to take greater risks in the effort to push for sanctions legislation from 1984 to 1986. Chapter 8 illustrates the way activists generated frames through which the public could focus on and interpret insurgency in South Africa and amplify expression of those concerns to policymakers. The conclusion summarizes the development of anti-apartheid activism, explores the movement's rapid decline, and addresses the theoretical implications of global interdependence for the study of activism.

Data sources for this project include organizational records, pamphlets, and publications of the American Committee on Africa; the Washington, D.C., Office on Africa; and newsletters of numerous local anti-apartheid support groups. Formal interviews with activists as well as statements from the journalistic and academic press and from congressional committee hearings have also been used.

Notes

1. Steven Metz, "The Anti-Apartheid Movement and the Populist Instinct in American Politics," *Political Science Quarterly* 101, 3 (Fall 1986):379–395.

2. "Free South Africa! New Life in an Old Movement: A Freedomways Report," *Freedomways* 25, 2 (Summer 1985):69–73.

3. Les de Villiers, *In Sight of Surrender: The U.S. Sanctions Campaign Against South Africa, 1946–1993* (New York: Praeger, 1995).

4. Brenda Gayle Plummer, *Rising Wind: Black Americans and U.S. Foreign Affairs, 1935–1960* (Chapel Hill: University of North Carolina Press, 1996).

5. Jan Aart Scholte, "From Power Politics to Social Change: An Alternative Focus for International Studies," *Review of International Studies* 19 (1993):3–21.

1

Interpreting Anti-Apartheid Activism

Numerous difficulties confront scholarly analysis of U.S. anti-apartheid activism. The movement's objectives, targets, action repertoire, longevity, and resource base resist easy description and analysis. From the sympathy marches of the early 1960s to the 1970s divestment drives and shantytown constructions in the 1980s, anti-apartheid activism assumed vastly different forms, depending upon the organizations involved, the resources available, and the linkages to other pressure groups.

Along with the challenge of determining which stages of the movement merit attention is the problem of selecting the most appropriate theoretical framework. Social movements represent a form of political participation that traditionally occurs when routine participation opportunities are limited. Stretching beyond the boundaries of conventional politics, social movements inject excluded issues and concerns into the political system through an extensive range of activities. A social movement is not a single organization pursuing its goals. As Warren Magnusson argues, movements tend to be:

1. *Plural:* There is not just one movement in any place, but many; individuals may be part of as many movements as they have energy for, and the number of simultaneous movements is in principle unlimited.
2. *Impermanent:* Movements only last as long as the enthusiasm for them—either they become bureaucratized, or they disappear.
3. *Inchoate:* Movements have no definite membership, authority relations, purposes, or programs.
4. *Inclusive:* In principle, anyone can be part of a movement, and there can be no definite means of excluding a person.
5. *Unbounded:* A movement takes in as many people, as much territory, as many issues as seem appropriate to the people involved.[1]

To avoid generalizations that undermine the utility of the concept, we must place in temporal and situational context the ways that social movements emerge and evolve into significant political forces. Social movement theory, just like theories that guide the study of other forms of interest representation,[2] must be lodged in an underlying theory of society, its major institutions and dynamics, and its material and ideational bases, as well as in assessments of what makes social movements possible. The remainder of the chapter presents a survey of social movement theories, their strengths and weaknesses, and the problems they pose for analysis of anti-apartheid activism.

Classical Theory

The dominant theories of social movements—classical models and resource mobilization, respectively—derive from different visions of society. Classical models explain the rise of social movements as a product of the breakdown of society's functional interdependence, established institutions, control mechanisms, and participatory channels. Proponents of this approach concentrate on change processes set in motion by structural transformation, including wars, economic change, and migration. Classical models posit a strong correlation between the levels of discomfort experienced by aggrieved segments of society and the emergence of collective action. They explain social movements as unusual moments when the social tensions experienced by participants find cathartic expression through collective action. Scholars from this tradition consequently treat movements as deviations from regular institutionalized political processes.[3]

Proponents of classical theory treat social movements as expressions of irrational behavior and make little effort to assess the impact of activism.[4] In most classical analyses, movements represent sudden eruptions within socially and political marginalized segments of the population, groups unlikely to exert meaningful influence on established institutions and practices. Classical approaches denounce citizen efforts to influence foreign policy as utopian or, at best, as extensions of the instrumentalist objective of charismatic leaders. This reinforces traditional biases that relegate public activism in foreign affairs to the margins of the policymaking environment.[5]

Resource Mobilization Theory

Resource mobilization theory originated in response to deficiencies in classical attempts to explain 1960s social activism. Leading proponents John McCarthy and Mayer Zald define social movements as "a set of opinions and beliefs in a population which represents preferences for changing some elements of the social structure and/or reward distribution of a society."[6] According to this view, the major obstacles faced by emergent groups are organizational. Studies guided by resource mobilization models consequently stress the efforts of marginalized groups to attract external resources and create new organizations.

Resource mobilization theory's focus on organization relies on Robert Salisbury's exchange theory, which uses economic concepts to evaluate interest groups.[7] From this perspective, entrepreneurial individuals play a key role in movement formation. As part of the process of initiating collective action, these individuals generate both material and intangible resources for use in recruiting members. Movement entrepreneurs may, for example, devise solidarity incentives—the benefits of friendship and camaraderie—to attract and retain followers. Resource mobilization theorists view the ensemble of such movement tactics as an alternative to normal politics for conventionally excluded groups seeking access to established political institutions.

Movement strength may grow as a result of successful appeals to established institutions and groups. When movements attract allies, develop communications networks, gather resources, and exercise entrepreneurial leadership, they are apt to exert political influence. If they do not connect with established groups, the likelihood of their making an impact diminishes. The prospects of movement success increase during periods of relative economic prosperity as organizations effectively commandeer discretionary resources from both elite and mass supporters. Individual organizations will self-advertise and cite their success to expand their share of resources and compete with other potential movements. The quality and quantity of resources, according to this view, will influence a movement's development.

Resource mobilization theorists stress how social movements considerably alter power relationships as a result of their organizational efforts. Challenging groups can secure policy successes by forcing changes in the content of official decisions, such as legislation or corporate investment and hiring policies. Insurgents can also gain by modifying the institutional practices that routinely define the decisionmaking procedures and agendas. Changes in the patterns and channels of elite socialization and recruitment, the articulation of new issues and perspectives, and the introduction of new rules defining legitimate actors and forms of collective action all provide opportunities for challengers to exert influence.

Since the 1970s, resource mobilization theory has guided research on such social movements as civil rights, feminism, and peace and environmental activism. It has also, however, generated substantial criticism. Bert Klandermans, for example, acknowledges the importance of

organizations and resources for social movements but contends that resource mobilization scholars focus too much on how social movements
are generated but neglect why they form.[8] Joyce Gelb and Marian Palley's study of the women's movement similarly suggests that organizational entrepreneurs and resources play only a secondary role in movement growth.[9] Both of these reservations question the extent to which
insurgent groups can generate resources and thereby reduce the costs of
participation in social movements without engaging in some initial form
of political action.

The emphasis on the organizational characteristics of social movements provokes criticisms about the role of external elite institutions as
patrons of activism. J. Craig Jenkins and Craig Eckert, in a study of black
insurgency during the civil rights era, found that elite sponsorship followed activism rather than generating it.[10] They further contend that elite
sponsorship seldom develops during the earliest stages, when movements desperately need resources. Similarly, David Meyer's analysis of
the nuclear freeze movement concluded that elite support is not con-
stant.[11] Alberto Melucci argues that by drawing too heavily from organizational theory and relying on market-based analysis, resource mobilization theory reduces everything to calculation, bargaining, and exchange,
while undervaluing the meanings and repercussion of political action.[12]
These critics stress the importance of examining the political character of
social movements, that is, how people interpret grievances, as well as
how they develop organizational resources to challenge them.

New Social Movements

A third approach, "new social movements," grew out of the intensification of activism in the 1980s, particularly in Western European countries.
New social movements models explain this rise of new groups and patterns of collective activity as a response to fundamental changes in
postindustrial societies. They emphasize the way structural changes in
advanced democracies have undermined the capacity of such societies to
produce basic levels of satisfaction for many segments of their populations. Economic instability; unemployment and underemployment;
rapidly diminishing levels of natural resources; rising economic, social,
and psychological costs of production; and a reduced capacity for crisis
management and problem solving serve as catalysts in the formation of
social movements.

Like classical models, new social movement approaches focus on ruptures in society that abet activism. In addressing one of the major criticisms of resource mobilization models, new social movement analysis focuses especially on the formation of collective identities as a response to

discontinuities generated by postindustrial development. Melucci explains collective identity as "an interactive and shared definition produced by several interacting individuals who are concerned with the orientations of their action as well as the field of opportunities and constraints in which their action takes place."[13] From this perspective, solidarity, which facilitates collective action, arises from active construction and is not merely a product of shared social spaces.

Although the new social movement paradigm concentrates on the rise of social movements in advanced capitalist societies, it bears some resemblance to classical theories, as it emphasizes the emergence of new values, action forms, and cultural critiques of modernity generated by economic restructuring processes, conflicts, and crises of postindustrial development. Indeed, critics such as William Gamson contend that the focus on a subset of social movement participants in Western Europe and North America deflects attention from similar collective identity processes in past movements and overlooks what might be instructive continuities between political activism across temporal, class, and geographical lines. Klandermans argues that the "new" perspective emphasizes social movement organizations as goals in themselves or as democratic enclaves in highly bureaucratic, corporatist societies, instead of examining how such groups pursue instrumentalist objectives. Last, although the new social movement theories illuminate shared problems that contribute to mobilization, scholars have made little effort to account more thoroughly for the common international origins of recent social movements.[14]

Political Process Theory

Another theory appears to offer an alternative to resource mobilization and new social movement models. The political process model presents a more comprehensive approach to the study of social movements by incorporating elements suggested by both solidarity and breakdown theories. It developed as a response to the inadequacies of resource mobilization theory, but it also corrects for some of the weaknesses of new social movement theory. Process theory directs attention to the way social movements develop as a function of changes within the established political system as well as within the aggrieved population. Scholars emphasize this interaction—the political opportunity structure[15]—as a crucial determinant in shaping conditions and resources that affect the direction and intensity of insurgent efforts.

This approach shares several features with resource mobilization. Advocates of both view social movements as politically oriented behavior and not simply as social-psychological means of reducing individual and group tensions. Second, both closely examine the linkages between movement organizations and groups external to them. There remain, nevertheless, some important distinctions. Whereas resource mobilization accords a significant role to elites in the social movement, the political process model more strongly privileges the insurgency of groups without formal or recognized power. Proponents question the probability that established elites would sponsor group activities that pose threats to entrenched interests.

The political process model shares with the new social movements approach an interest in the changing consciousness of movement participants. Yet proponents of the latter emphasize the construction of a collective identity that emerges from a new value system, or a break with the dominant goal structure of society. Scholars using the process theory focus on identifying the political changes that let activists know when established institutions have become more vulnerable to change. Those cognitive cues produce evidence that warrants reinterpretation of established relationships and the projection of new strategies. An appreciation for continuity is perhaps the model's most enduring feature. Doug McAdam contends that "a movement represents a continuous process from generation to decline, rather than a discrete series of development stages. Accordingly, any complete model of social insurgency should offer the researcher a framework for analyzing the entire process of movement development rather than a particular phase of that same process."[16]

Research guided by a political process approach focuses on three factors crucial to the generation of social movement activity: the structure of political opportunity, organizational readiness, and the level of consciousness and confidence within the movement. The opportunity structure refers to the ensemble of the political climate and institutional policies of the state and major private sector interests that movements seek to challenge. Disruptive processes such as large-scale demographic transitions, industrialization, electoral realignment, prolonged unemployment, and wars influence the character of the political opportunity structure.[17]

The second element crucial to the success of a social movement is an organizational structure that transforms fragmented energies into concrete weapons for change. Unlike traditional theories that focus on charismatic leadership, the political process model attaches greater weight to how the social movement articulates its goals, whether it espouses single or multiple objectives, and the quality and availability of resources. Indicators of organization type include the degree of bureaucratization, centralization, and factionalism; the mobilization strategies used; and the strategic location of members.

The third element in the political process model is an insurgent consciousness, or cognitive liberation.[18] This explains how organizations and participants interpret favorable shifts in political opportunity in ways that mobilize broader communities of supporters to engage in collective action. The subjective meanings that people attach to day-to-day occurrences convey information about how they assess the prospects for successful collective protest.[19] Such dramatic events as elections, court decisions, or wars may communicate this information, but so do less stirring developments, such as provision of new administrative resources, formation of advisory groups, or the opening of new channels of access by potential allies. The onus nevertheless falls upon movement participants to recognize when established institutions are becoming more receptive to challenges.

Toward a Revised Political Process Model

The political process approach overcomes many of the limitations of resource mobilization and new social movements models because it allows exploration of the origins, development, and consequences of social movements. Exclusive concentration on state-movement interaction, however, disguises the political processes that help create such phenomena as anti-apartheid activism. The state-centered political process approach relies upon a representation of power as a dyadic relation between ruler and subject. From this perspective, power constitutes possession of convertible resources such as money, administrative capacity, the use of force, or legal authority, which enable a group to maintain dominance or control. Implicit in this representation is the idea that power, held by challengers or the state, develops in a linear, cumulative fashion. This approach reinforces realist assumptions in studies of American–South African relations that cede little or no role for opposition movements.[20] It furthermore obscures the impact of more subtle elements of conflict, uncertainty, and failure as both state and oppositional strategies develop.

Research on the dynamics of welfare state capitalism provides further incentive to develop a more thorough grasp of state–social movement linkages. The institutionalization of state regulation of private economic activity has weakened distinctions between public and private sectors. Recent studies have emphasized the way state preemption of public conflicts with private sector interests contributes to the gradual depoliticization of public life. They thus afford a view of power as a relationship rather than a possession.[21]

The development of the welfare state apparatus during World War II provided a basis for stabilizing major conflicts that previously disrupted capitalist production.[22] Enlargement of the state's reach, however, seldom continued without contradiction or interruption. Administrative and fiscal requirements for optimizing private capital accumulation and assuring basic levels of need satisfaction for citizens invariably provoked public discussion about the collective sacrifices entailed. The consequent repoliticization of the public sphere illuminates the state's place as a critical site of contestation. Yet the power of the transformed state resides less in traditional instruments such as monopoly on the use of force and violence and increasingly in its soft power: its capacity to legitimize the claims of other actors and its need to preserve and extend its own legitimacy.[23]

As the above discussion suggests, this book rejects the inert state-centric model of the political process and replaces it with analysis of the complex state-society-movement interactions that emerged in response to postindustrial transformation and global interdependence. Instead, it attempts to locate and explore how these transition processes set in motion new resources, social groups, targets, and trajectories of activism. In doing so, it paints an alternative picture of anti-apartheid activism in which the movement emerges from a series of struggles within and beyond state- and private-sector institutions, struggles that forced institutional decisionmakers to revise their strategies for maintaining racial inequality in South Africa.

These encounters also illustrate the ongoing character of postindustrialist adjustment. They further demonstrate that globalization exists not just "out there" but is embedded in the fabric of American society, institutions, and political practice. Three elements of this process—structural economic changes that enhanced the role of critical expertise; the expansion of the sociodemographic base of activism; and the diffusion of social movement issues, technology, catalysts, resources, and constituencies across national borders—offer insights into the shifting locale of anti-apartheid concerns in the United States.

Scholars have widely acknowledged the contributions of scientific and technological advances to economic growth, but only in recent years have they devoted significant attention to how these developments affect the climate of social movement formation. Zald contends that there has been a rise of movements, such as environmental protectionism and opposition to nuclear power, that respond to the negative externalities of industrial growth. Karl-Werner Brand maintains that cultural critiques of modernity, which historically accompany periods of modernization, have intensified in post–World War II Western societies. Similarly, Timothy Luke argues that critical intellectuals continue to play vital roles in an information-based society.[24] These studies suggest that the politicization of expertise, whether interpreted as esotericism, the ability to define issues and evaluate facts, or as the possession of intervention skills, enhances movement efforts to access discursive and policymaking arenas.

The development of African studies in the United States illustrates how critical expertise develops linkages to a social movement. The postwar revitalization of area studies, largely undertaken by major foundations and the federal government, evolved from the need to expand America's institutional capacity to address rapid decolonization. Funded graduate programs, professional development initiatives, conferences, learned associations, and journals created and sustained networks of proficient Africanists. The field included scholars from a range of social science disciplines and from the humanities and applied sciences. Africanists, like members of other professional networks, subsequently influenced a growing American awareness of Africa and provided empirical validation of the claims made by anti-apartheid activists.[25]

The major growth stage of African studies programs occurred between 1960 and 1970. More than thirty programs offered advanced degrees in African studies by 1970, and nearly fifty other institutions provided undergraduate majors or concentrations in African studies. The growth of development studies enabled professional Africanists to establish an identity that distinguished them from earlier generations of Americans who had an interest in Africa. Yet these developments in no way produced consensus within the field about the mission of African studies, as is indicated by conflicts such as those that emerged at the 1969 African Studies Association meetings in Montreal.[26] The intellectual vitality of African studies nevertheless constituted a key factor in enhancing the credibility of Africanist scholars in the policymaking arena.

Africanists began to experience regular opportunities for applying their critical expertise to policy issues in 1969 when Michigan representative Charles C. Diggs assumed the chair of the House Subcommittee on Africa in Congress. His leadership, primarily evident in hearings that focused on U.S. policy toward southern Africa, provided a crucial opportunity for anti-apartheid forces to develop stronger links with segments of the policymaking community that opposed Nixon administration efforts to build closer relations with the settler-dominated states in the region. Subcommittee on Africa hearings provided an occasion for new participants in the policymaking arena to express policy preferences and demonstrate the policy salience of their expertise. The subcommittee became more active after 1969 and expanded the range of witnesses who provided testimony. Anti-apartheid groups and academic Africanists especially benefited from this opening. The changing character of the witness pool also reflects the enhanced role of committee staff that resulted from congressional reorganization in the early 1970s. Since 1973, the staff director of the Subcommittee on Africa and the majority of the five-person staff have been academically trained Africanists. The evolution of an activist posture on the subcommittee's part provided an opportunity to expand the interested public and enhance the legitimacy of anti-apartheid perspectives.[27]

The similarly increased visibility of human rights groups in the policy-making community coincided with the unfolding of American–southern African crises and augmented the human rights component of anti-apartheid activism. Human rights groups, besides offering their testimony at congressional committee hearings, provided legal assistance to southern African refugees seeking political asylum, channeled financial and legal resources to attorneys representing political dissidents in South Africa, challenged the legality of the South African government's stateside commercial ventures, and initiated domestic litigation to force U.S. courts to recognize international human rights laws.[28] Although the origins of Africanist human rights advocacy date to the late nineteenth century in the United States, the maturing expertise of such groups, and their concomitant political influence, grew out of a convergence of factors that accompanied American adjustment to global interdependence after World War II. The growth of higher education in area studies and international law underwrote the proliferation of professional groups whose core experiences and values involve interaction with the global community. Employment for graduates of these programs generated concentrations of skilled professional internationalists, not just in proximity to policymaking institutions in Washington, D.C., and New York City but also around state capitals and in college and university communities.[29]

Several other demographic factors are pertinent here. They include changes in the racial-ethnic character of the nation's population, increased rates of female participation in the labor force and in higher education, and the breakdown of the linear life course. The changing racial composition of postwar society exerted significant influence on the efforts of previously marginalized minorities such as African Americans, Latinos, Asian and Native Americans to legitimate their standing, gain access to the polity, and secure voting rights. The politicization of these groups, especially in urban areas and in regions with significant concentrations of non-Europeans and political refugees, led to the creation of new coalitions and collective self-definitions.[30] Groups emerged within those communities to challenge policies oriented toward their international constituents, as well as toward traditionally defined domestic at-risk constituencies. Blacks, for example, used electoral gains of the civil rights era to form Africa-issue organizations and institutionalize their foreign policy concerns about the Caribbean and Africa.[31]

Increased involvement of women in the labor force and in higher education led to the politicization of activities, issues, and concerns previously confined to the margins of the economy. The women's movement created new resources for contesting traditional patterns of exclusion in professional as well as blue-collar workplaces.[32] In many of these settings, women not only joined but also assisted in the redefinition of workplace agendas and the creation of new standards of behavior. The ample representation of women as leaders in a wide range of anti-apartheid organizations and as staff members of the House Subcommittee on Africa, demonstrates the openness of movement constituencies to gender equity.

Changes in the linear life course expectations by men and women furnished additional opportunities for expanding the base of social movements. The family wage system, once identified as fundamental to industrial society, proved no longer viable. Prolonged and interrupted career preparation; delayed or altered family formation patterns; reliance upon part-time, temporary, or cyclical employment; flexible work and leisure time; and greater concentrations of highly trained, urban-based populations expanded the potential membership base for social movements during an era when the American workplace began to adjust to the changes accelerated by globalization of the economy.[33] The changing demands of the workplace and family life enabled substantial segments of the population to channel more time into nonelectoral political activity.

Traditionally, social movement scholars focus on "at-risk" populations as the base for social movement formation. At-risk groups consisted of those segments of the population viewed as most vulnerable to economic instability or those experiencing low levels of social mobility and assimilation. Scholars also distinguish between beneficiary constituencies that would profit directly from the achievement of movement objectives and conscience constituencies that are motivated to participate by the desire to alleviate adverse conditions suffered by aggrieved populations. The sociodemographic changes noted above have contributed to the blurring of distinctions between the two constituencies and have thus enlarged the mobilizable population for social movement activity.[34]

Finally, one of the most significant by-products of global interdependence is the cross-fertilization of social movements, which have greater opportunities to share ideas, resources, strategies, and symbols. Technological developments in media and information dissemination make it possible for movements in one society to have demonstration effects on citizens in other countries and to reinforce relationships and networks that emerge from professional, educational, cultural, and political interactions. U.S. anti-apartheid activists relied heavily upon long-term relationships with southern African liberation movements, as well as on alliances with European anti-apartheid organizations. More recently, technological innovation played a substantial role in facilitating social movement growth as organizations adopted new techniques of fund-raising and constituency identification. The computer revolution facilitated use of mass-mail marketing techniques. Similarly, the use of professional fund-raisers, canvassers, and telephone solicitation—conventionally the tools of establishment politics—expanded the potential base of support.[35]

The transformations of the welfare state and the global political economy encouraged a shift from studying isolated movements to analyzing the totality of movement activity in society. Roberta Garner and Mayer Zald argue that this configuration of movements in advanced industrial societies constitutes a social movement sector.[36] The components and determinants of the social movement sector warrant further discussion.

Components include the size of social movements compared to other group representation forms, the degree of organization within movements, the social location of movement support, movement alignments within the left-right political spectrum, the autonomy of movements from other sectors, and the character of change within the movement sector over time. Historically, the idiosyncrasies of America's state administrative apparatus and political party system afforded citizens substantial independent mobilization space around nonpoliticized religious, lifestyle, and regional issues. The nationalization of the economy, particularly after the New Deal, led not only to the expanded reach of state bureaucracies and political parties but also to encroachments on previously unaligned issues and constituencies by other national institutions such as labor unions, interest groups, foundations, universities, and media.[37] Although issues such as civil rights for women and minorities effectively penetrated the postwar national political system, adjustments to postindustrialization and global interdependence highlight environmental, human rights, and foreign policy problems that have thus far resisted incorporation and co-optation.

The second element of the social movement sector—its determinants—defines the manner in which the dynamics of the political economy constrain and facilitate opportunities for movement development. The political economy and its attendant social relationships exert significant influence on the types of cleavages that emerge in society and affect the distribution of the material resources that groups use to engage in and sustain political struggle. Unlike traditional approaches, which concentrate on the class composition of movement organizations, this study examines changes in the broader structure of productive relations—the shift from industrial to postindustrial activities, relations between the public and private sectors, the nature of work relations, and the political associations that develop from work arrangements. It explores how postindustrial, globally interdependent development substantially altered the material and ideational bases for anti-apartheid activity.

The political system, viewed apart from global economic forces, also has a separate and independent effect. It acts as a mechanism for filtering and mediating conflicts and tensions between established institutions and social movements. The types of civil liberties afforded social movements, for example, shape the strategies chosen by activists and clarify the co-optation and management potential of mainstream institutions. The state, the party, interest groups, and other entrenched structures often provide regulated space for the domestication of unaligned issues. This book will demonstrate that anti-apartheid activists capitalized on a political system weakened by activist surges of the late 1960s, profited from declining public confidence in established institutions following the Watergate scandals, and benefited from uncertainty about the national role in the post-Vietnam world community.

Conclusion

The contextualized political process approach, with its focus on the pivotal role of political factors in determining the timing and prospects for social movement development, offers a viable theory for understanding the development of U.S. anti-apartheid activism. The movement emerged from shifting power configurations in southern Africa, among nongovernmental groups in the United States and abroad, and within international governmental organizations such as NATO, the European Community, the Commonwealth nations, the United Nations, and the International Court of Justice.[38] Because the maintenance of apartheid relied on a complex international network of financial, military, technological, and managerial associations, mobilization against its injustices required not only mounting challenges to U.S. government and corporate policy toward South Africa but also uncovering the matrix of domestic linkages to the system of racial inequality.

Movement success derived from an expanding structure of political opportunity rather than from entrepreneurial skills in commandeering resources from elites. Thus, the three components of political process theory used to analyze the development of the anti-apartheid movement are: widening of political spaces and opportunity for mobilizing around apartheid; group enlistment of material and symbolic resources; and increased confidence and empowerment of organizations, their members, and their supporters.

Notes

1. Warren Magnusson, "The Reification of Political Community," in R.B.J. Walker and Saul H. Mendlovitz, eds., *Contending Sovereignties: Redefining Political Community* (Boulder: Lynne Rienner, 1990), p. 52.

2. Jeffrey Berry, *The Interest Group Society*, 2d ed. (New York: HarperCollins, 1989).

3. Aldon Morris and Cedric Herring, "Theory and Research in Social Movements: A Critical Review," in *Annual Review of Political Science*, vol. 2 (Norwood, N.J.: Ablex, 1987), pp. 155–158.

4. J. Craig Jenkins, *The Politics of Insurgency: The Farm Worker Movement in the 1960s* (New York: Columbia University Press, 1985), p. 21.

5. Charles Kegley and Eugene Wittkopf, *The Domestic Sources of American Foreign Policy* (New York: St. Martin's Press, 1988).

6. John McCarthy and Mayer Zald, "Resource Mobilization and Social Movements: A Partial Theory," *American Journal of Sociology* 82 (May 1977):1217–1218.

7. Robert Salisbury, "An Exchange Theory of Interest Groups," *Midwest Journal of Political Science* 13 (1969):1–32.

8. Bert Klandermans, "The Peace Movement and Social Movement Theory," in *International Social Movement Research*, vol. 3 (Greenwich, Conn.: JAI Press, 1991), pp. 5–6.

9. Joyce Gelb and Marian Palley, *Women and Public Policies* (Princeton: Princeton University Press, 1982).

10. J. Craig Jenkins and Craig M. Eckert, "Channeling Black Insurgency: Elite Patronage and Professional Social Movement Organizations in the Development of the Black Movement," *American Sociological Review* 51 (December 1986): 812–829.

11. David Meyer, *A Winter of Nuclear Discontent: The Nuclear Freeze and American Politics* (New York: Praeger, 1990), p. 7.

12. Alberto Melucci, *Nomads of the Present: Social Movements and Individual Needs in Contemporary Society* (Philadelphia: Temple, 1990), p. 194.

13. Ibid., p. 34.

14. Russell J. Dalton and Manfred Kuechler, eds., *Challenging the Political Order: New Social and Political Movements in Western Democracies* (New York: Oxford University Press, 1990), pp. 4–10; William Gamson, "The Social Psychology of Collective Action," in Aldon D. Morris and Carol McClurg Mueller, eds., *Frontiers in Social Movement Theory* (New Haven: Yale University Press, 1992), p. 59; Klandermans, "The Peace Movement," pp. 5–6; Jan Aart Scholte, "From Power Politics to Social Change: An Alternative Focus for International Studies," *Review of International Studies* 19 (1993):3–21.

15. Charles Tilly, *From Mobilization to Revolution* (Reading, Mass.: Addison-Wesley, 1978); Sidney Tarrow, *Struggling to Reform: Social Movements and Policy Change During Cycles of Protest* (Ithaca: Cornell Studies in International Affairs, 1983).

16. Doug McAdam, *Political Process and the Development of Black Insurgency, 1930–1970* (Chicago: University of Chicago Press, 1982), p. 36.

17. Robert L. Allen, *Reluctant Reformers: Racism and Social Reform Movements in the United States* (Washington, D.C.: Howard University Press, 1983); Jenkins, *The Politics of Insurgency*; Aldon D. Morris, *The Origins of the Civil Rights Movement: Black Communities Organizing for Change* (New York: Free Press, 1984).

18. McAdam, *Political Process*, pp. 48–51.

19. Murray Edelman, *Politics as Symbolic Action* (Chicago: Markham Press, 1971).

20. Iris Marion Young, *Justice and the Politics of Difference* (Princeton: Princeton University Press, 1990), pp. 31–32; Peter J. Schraeder, *United States Foreign Policy Toward Africa: Incrementalism, Crisis, and Change* (New York: Cambridge University Press, 1994).

21. Jürgen Habermas, *The Theory of Communicative Competence: Lifeworld and System* (Boston: Beacon, 1987), pp. 343–345; Michel Foucault, *Discipline and Punish* (New York: Pantheon, 1977).

22. Fred Block, *Revising State Theory: Essays in Politics and Postindustrialism* (Philadelphia: Temple University Press, 1987).

23. Joseph Nye Jr., *Bound to Lead: The Changing Nature of American Power* (New York: Basic Books, 1990), pp. 174–201; Tilly, *From Mobilization to Revolution*.

24. Mayer N. Zald, "The Trajectory of Social Movements in America," in *Research in Social Movements, Conflict, and Change* vol. 10 (Greenwich, Conn.: JAI Press, 1988), p. 25; Karl-Werner Brand, "Cyclical Aspects of New Social Movements: Waves of Cultural Criticism and Mobilization Cycles of New Middle-Class Radicalism," in Dalton and Kuechler, eds., *Challenging the Political Order*, p. 23; Frances McCrea and Gerald Markle, "Atomic Scientists and Protests," in *Research in Social Movements, Conflict, and Change,* vol. 11 (Greenwich, Conn.: JAI Press, 1989), pp. 219–233; Timothy W. Luke, *Screens of Power: Ideology, Domination, and Resistance in Informational Society* (Urbana and Chicago: University of Illinois Press, 1989), pp. 207–239.

25. Kevin Danaher, *Beyond Safaris: A Guide to Building People-to-People Ties with Africa* (Trenton, N.J.: Africa World Press, 1991); Brenda Gayle Plummer, *Rising Wind: Black Americans and U.S. Foreign Affairs, 1935–1960* (Chapel Hill: University of North Carolina Press, 1996).

26. *Directory of African and Afro-American Studies Programs,* 7th ed. (Waltham, Mass.: Crossroads Press, 1987); Pearl T. Robinson and Elliott P. Skinner, eds., *Transformation and Resiliency in Africa* (Washington, D.C.: Howard University Press, 1983), pp. 3–26; Martin Staniland, "Who Needs African Studies?" *African Studies Review* 26, 3–4 (September–December 1983):77–97.

27. *Congressional Staff Directory* (Mt. Vernon, Va.: Congressional Staff Directory Limited, 1958–1990); James A. Thurber, "Dynamics of Policy Subsystems in American Politics," in Allan J. Cigler and Burdett A. Loomis, eds., *Interest Group Politics* (Washington, D.C.: Congressional Quarterly Press, 1991), pp. 330–333.

28. Howard Tolley Jr., "Interest Group Litigation to Enforce Human Rights," *Political Science Quarterly* 105, 4 (Winter 1990–1991):620–623.

29. Edward Berman, *The Influence of the Carnegie, Ford, and Rockefeller Foundations on American Foreign Policy: The Ideology of Philanthropy* (Albany: SUNY Press, 1983); Robert McCaughey, *International Studies and Academic Enclosure: A Chapter in the Enclosure of American Learning* (New York: Columbia University Press, 1984); Michael McCann, *Taking Reform Seriously: Perspectives on Public Interest Liberalism* (Ithaca: Cornell University Press, 1986).

30. Zald, "Trajectory of Social Movements," p. 28.

31. Elliott P. Skinner, "African American Perspectives on Foreign Policy," in Linda F. Williams and Ralph Gomes, eds., *From Exclusion to Inclusion: The African American Struggle for Political Power* (Westport, Conn.: Greenwood Press, 1992), pp. 173–186.

32. Guida West and Rhoda Blumberg, eds., *Women and Social Protest* (New York: Oxford University Press, 1990); Anne Costain, "Social Movements as Interest Groups: The Case of the Women's Movement," in Mark P. Petracca, ed., *The Politics of Interests: Interest Groups Transformed* (Boulder: Westview Press, 1992), pp. 285–287.

33. Claus Offe, "New Social Movements: Changing Boundaries of the Political," *Social Research* 52 (1985):832–838.

34. McCarthy and Zald, "Resource Mobilization," pp. 1212–1239; Fred Block, *Postindustrial Possibilities: A Critique of Economic Discourse* (Berkeley and Los Angeles: University of California Press, 1990), p. 10.

35. Klandermans, "The Peace Movement," pp. 11–12; Medea Benjamin and Andrea Freedman, *Bridging the Global Gap: A Handbook to Linking Citizens of the First and Third Worlds* (Cabin John, Md.: Seven Locks Press, 1989); Chadwick Alger, "Grassroots Perspectives on Global Policies for Development," *Journal of Peace Research* 27, 2 (1990):155–168; Abdul S. Minty, "The Anti-Apartheid Movement and Racism in Southern Africa," in Peter Willetts, ed., *Pressure Groups in the Global System: The Transnational Relations of Issue-Oriented Non-Governmental Organizations* (New York: St. Martin's Press, 1982), pp. 28–45; "Drive for Divestment Red Hot!" *Washington Notes on Africa* (Spring 1983):6; Berry, *The Interest Group Society*, pp. 61–66; Meyer, *A Winter of Discontent*, pp. 182–183.

36. Roberta Garner and Mayer Zald, "The Political Economy of Social Movement Sectors," in Mayer N. Zald and John D. McCarthy, eds., *Social Movements in an Organizational Society: Selected Essays* (New Brunswick, N.J.: Transaction Books, 1987), pp. 293–319.

37. Stephen Skowronek, *Building a New American State: The Expansion of the National Administrative Capacity* (New York: Cambridge University Press, 1982).

38. George Shepherd, *Anti-Apartheid: Transnational Conflict and Western Policy in the Liberation of South Africa* (Westport, Conn.: Greenwood Press, 1977).

2

Discovery, Dependence, and Denial: The Legacy of U.S.–South African Relations, 1867–1960

Understanding anti-apartheid activism from 1960 to 1987 requires an analysis of U.S.–South African relations that addresses the domestic and international contexts that endowed these relations, the power and values derived from mutual exchanges, and the opportunities and vulnerabilities that confronted the participants as the relationship evolved. Power facilitates the introduction of some issues into the political process, which simultaneously pushes other issues out. As E. E. Schattschneider wrote, the study of politics must focus "both on who gets what, when and how, and who gets left out and how."[1]

This perspective on power can benefit from a historical survey of South African–American relations. Since the late nineteenth century, American citizen groups had appealed to the federal government to challenge the violent racial policies of colonial and settler-dominated regimes in South Africa. Although their concerns did not begin to penetrate domestic debate until the Sharpeville massacre of 1960, their protests took place against a backdrop of expanding opportunity for American economic and political interests.

This chapter examines three critical stages in the evolving U.S. engagement with South Africa: The first begins with the 1867 discovery of diamonds in Kimberly and ends with the Boer War in 1902. The second originates in the postwar unification of South Africa and concludes with the depression of the late 1920s. The third stage starts with the 1930s rejuvenation of the American–South African connection and lasts until political tensions associated with the ruling National Party's 1960 efforts to solidify the apartheid system drew international condemnation. Each period presented opportunities for advancing U.S. objectives, but each step in the relationship enhanced U.S. vulnerability to criticism as it exposed the contradictions between democratic principles and pragmatic foreign policies. The chapter concludes with an assessment of two early anti-apartheid organizations, the Council on African Affairs and Americans for South African Resistance.

Public debate about U.S. economic involvement with South Africa intensified after the Sharpeville massacre in 1960, but the relationship between the two countries goes back nearly three centuries. For most of that period, the American constituency on South Africa consisted only of small groups of businessmen, diplomats, and missionaries. Concern with the institutionalization and expansion of the system of racial domination throughout southern Africa thus rarely penetrated public consciousness.

American Business Penetration and South Africa's "Western Frontier," 1867–1899

During the final third of the nineteenth century, economic structural developments in the United States and South Africa profoundly altered each country's linkages to the world economy and provided a foundation for broadening mutual political, business, and cultural connections. The United States emerged from the Civil War with new industrial and communications technologies that transformed it into a regional power. The discovery in South Africa of vast reserves of diamonds in 1867 and gold in 1886 intensified the struggle among the European colonial powers to exploit this new source of mineral wealth. The United States enjoyed only limited direct ties to Africa but possessed several advantages that enabled it to greatly influence the development of mining and act as a major sponsor of South Africa's integration into the capitalist world economy. The California gold rush experience of 1848 and the development of mining operations throughout other Western states enabled the U.S. mining industry to evolve into one of the world's most advanced. Thousands of American engineers, technicians, and consultants provided the knowledge and skills that laid the foundations for South Africa's profitable extractive industry.[2]

American entrepreneurs used their base in mining to penetrate other sectors of the South African economy, creating, for example, Johannesburg's first municipal transportation system in 1891 and developing citrus plantations and wineries.[3] U.S. companies also gained a sizable share of the South African market in consumer goods and heavy industrial equipment. Many successful stateside companies went on to form manufacturing subsidiaries in South Africa.

South Africa in 1900 was not an independent country but rather a fragile union of the British-controlled Cape Colony and two independent Boer republics—the Orange Free State and the Transvaal. Tensions between the Boers and the British—both within the Cape Colony and in the republics—had been high since 1806, when the latter acquired control of the cape from the Dutch. These conflicts were not the sole political concern of American entrepreneurs in southern Africa. They faced competition from Germany, with its protectorate, South-West Africa (present-day Namibia), and Portugal, with colonies in neighboring Mozambique and Angola. American businesses played an integral part in South Africa's economic development and could not escape the political entanglements of the region.

North American business executives, though generally opposed to European imperialism, developed effective working relationships with Cecil Rhodes and other British capitalists. Deference to British dominance in South Africa also derived from the assumption that reciprocal respect would accompany American hegemony on the other side of the Atlantic.[4] American businessmen furthermore viewed the Boers, descendants of mid-seventeenth-century Dutch settlers, as crude, corrupt, inefficient, and narrowly exploitative of Africa's natural resources and people. In contrast, British imperialism combined a missionary ethos with economic objectives. U.S. entrepreneurs and missionaries developed a special collaborative relationship with the British in South Africa. They were less successful with the Boers, who remained suspicious of the foreign influx accompanying the country's rapid economic growth.[5]

British-Boer conflict escalated into full-scale war in 1899. The Boer War presented a dilemma for the U.S. government. As a result of widespread international opposition to British imperialism, the U.S. attitude toward the war became especially important to Britain. The Republican administration of William McKinley, though officially neutral, remained friendly to Britain. Once registered in public consciousness at home, however, the war revealed disagreement with official policy among certain popular sectors. Many American citizens, particularly immigrants from traditionally Anglophobic Ireland, Germany, and the Netherlands, sympathized with the Boers. The 1900 Democratic Party platform, moreover, courted the same ethnic constituencies and included anti-British planks. Finally, Boer lobbyists in the United States actively cultivated supporters in large cities along the East Coast.[6]

Imperial Adjustment and Dependent Development in South Africa, 1903–1929

The position that both McKinley and the succeeding administration of Theodore Roosevelt took on the Boer War was partly motivated by the belief that a British victory would present greater opportunities for American business penetration of South African markets. U.S. companies remained optimistic that they would gain access to the Orange Free State and the Transvaal and accelerate the entry of black African workers and consumers into a larger, national market. But by the end of the war, the United States had replaced Germany as Britain's chief commercial rival. Britain subsequently began a protectionist drive in 1903 that resulted in increasing the costs of U.S. business operations in South Africa, while simultaneously restricting access to colonial territories. U.S. companies faced an array of barriers—a permit system, exclusion from the bidding on rail and mining construction projects, more red tape for American imports, cancellation of contracts—that decreased the attractiveness of their goods in the South African market. South Africa at the same time began a rebate system that subsidized British-produced goods.

Prospects did not improve until 1910, with the establishment of the Union of South Africa. Non-Europeans (i.e., Africans and Asians) were excluded from political participation. A coalition of Afrikaner and English-speaking parties gained control of the Union government and immediately began pushing trade beyond imperial boundaries. Receptivity to American business improved. The rejuvenation and rapid development of the South African connections of multinational corporations such as Standard Oil, Texaco, General Motors (GM), Ford, International Harvester, Firestone, and Goodyear resulted in part from successful antitrust actions in the United States that facilitated multinational expansion. This enabling legislation infused corporations with new capital for expansion.

The expansion of commerce with South Africa also included the film and tourist industries. A film distribution network established itself in South Africa in 1910, when American entrepreneur I. W. Schlesinger opened the first chain of privately owned radio stations there. U.S. tourism to South Africa began in 1926, and two years later, the American Express Company initiated tours to the Union.

The improved picture for U.S. commerce after 1910 accompanied the shift of trade-promotion issues from the State Department to the Commerce Department. Pressures from the business community for more opportunities abroad resulted in Congress passing the Federal Reserve Act of 1913, the Webb Pomerene Act of 1918, the Edge Act of 1919, and the Merchant Marine Act of 1920. These laws successfully accomplished what their creators had intended: the enhancement of the competitiveness of domestic firms abroad. World War I further enhanced opportunities for American trade with South Africa when fighting in Europe disrupted the flow of goods from Britain to the Union.[7]

Despite the growing intimacy in commercial and diplomatic relations between the two countries, American private-sector and government representatives assigned to South Africa remained oblivious to the flood of racially segregationist laws that issued from the new Union government beginning in 1911. American missionaries welcomed the opportunity to spread Christianity and provide education to indigenous Africans. For their part, white South Africans looked to the United States, particularly the Southern states, for guidance on how to control Africans.[8] The programs of Booker T. Washington, especially that of the Tuskegee Institute, attracted South African administrators and educators and produced several attempts to duplicate them in African communities. Washington's accommodationist philosophy seemed to many South Africans to hold the key to the future. The Tuskegee philosophy would modernize Africans while creating a subordinate role for them in the economy. They would develop socially along separate lines and, like African Americans in the post-Reconstruction American South, abstain from political participation.

Booker T. Washington's ideas enjoyed enlarged support among white South Africans when black American missionaries from the African Methodist Episcopal Church (AME) and the Ethiopian Movement came under suspicion because of their political activities.[9] Black American missionaries shared a special bond with Africans, as both labored under European-dominated institutions. South African race relations caused particular problems for black Americans in South Africa—visitors of color—as the experiences of AME church workers exemplify.

The AME church began its African mission in the early nineteenth century, employing proselytization to facilitate African adaptation to the changes caused by Western domination. The church used its southern African programs to extend Pan-Africanist ideals of racial advancement. The latent nationalism in this approach intensified as white control of African churches and the development of all-too-familiar patterns of race relations encouraged black American missionary identification with the independent, or Ethiopianist, church movement. African-American missionaries aggressively promoted African land ownership claims and political rights. They attempted to assert their own rights as U.S. citizens and challenged the restrictions of South African segregation laws. Black Americans in South Africa appealed for assistance to their diplomatic representatives there but were reminded that the U.S. Constitution had no force in a foreign country.[10] The South African government frequently responded to their complaints with expulsion.

Once white settlers achieved autonomy following the 1910 formation of the Union, all American missionaries had to reassess their South African operations. Large tracts of land, once controlled by missionaries and leased to African farmers, gradually came under Union administration, thus substantially reducing opportunities to successfully proselytize. American missionaries and philanthropists began to make educational programs part of their "civilizing" mission. The Phelps-Stokes Fund surveyed schooling in Africa and made recommendations to missionary societies and colonial governments. The fund's recommendations for Africans were invariably influenced by the pedagogical practices and philosophy of Tuskegee. As a model for Africans, Booker T. Washington's belief that blacks should strive for a practical, vocationally oriented education and rural self-sufficiency proved more attractive to colonialists than the notion that they should seek political and social equality with whites.[11]

Although Booker T. Washington's philosophy for black development resonated with the desires of white missionaries and philanthropists for docile Christians and those of the South African government for a quiescent peasantry, they drew sharp criticism from politically active segments of the African-American community. The National Association for the Advancement of Colored People (NAACP), a source of inspiration for the founders of the African National Congress (ANC), feared that South African interest in Washington's programs concealed interest in developing more severe forms of racial segregation. W.E.B. Du Bois, editor of the organization's journal *Crisis*, argued that the Union of South Africa sought to emulate the violent and repressive system of race relations in the American South.[12]

The Universal Negro Improvement Association (UNIA), founded by Marcus Garvey, generated enthusiastic followings in South Africa, especially in the Cape Province during the early 1920s. Garvey's slogan "Africa for Africans" and the theme of cultural confidence and solidarity contrasted strongly with Booker T. Washington's advocacy of compliance.[13] The UNIA produced only a few active chapters in South Africa, but as an alternative to the prevailing colonial ideology, it played an active role in shaping African political consciousness during the interwar period.

Carter G. Woodson, editor of the *Journal of Negro History*, accused the Phelps-Stokes Fund and its African Educational Commission of attempting to establish a system of education in Africa oriented toward extending colonial rule. Woodson also felt that extension of the Tuskegee philosophy would create a politically docile African working class. Criticism of American involvement with European colonialism in Africa also emerged from scholars such as Harvard anthropologist Raymond Leslie Buell, who wrote *The Native Problem in Africa* (1928), a study of the problems of colonial administration, and from Columbia University anthropologist Franz Boas, who wrote the first major scientific attack against theories of racial inequality and white supremacy. Although the work of these individual scholars provided intellectual reinforcement for critics of colonialism, the results of more rigorous investigation of African societies did not begin to appear in American anthropology textbooks until the 1930s. The first African studies program was established by Lorenzo Turner at Fisk University in the early 1940s, and a second was founded in 1948 by Melville Herskovitz at Northwestern University. However, the influence of scholarship remained limited in a society that expended few resources studying other parts of the world, and almost nothing on Africa.[14]

Between 1910, when the Union was formed, and 1929, when the Great Depression began, Americans interaction with South Africa rebounded from the protectionist practices set in motion just after the Boer War. U.S. corporations, diplomats, missionaries, educators, and philanthropists could participate in a rapidly maturing industrial economy as a result of the postwar availability of surplus capital and Union government strategies designed to lessen dependence on the British. The society in which resident white Americans were most comfortable was far removed from the black African world. Most expatriates knew little and cared less about the impact of racial domination and economic oppression on the majority of South Africa's people.

Rediscovery and Denial, 1930–1960

Historically, South Africa's enormous mineral wealth, combined with a peculiar network of external relationships, enabled it to maintain some degree of insulation from trends that sweep the world. Such was the case in the early 1930s when the strong price of gold insulated the country from the full force of the worldwide depression. As a result, its extractive industries experienced another major expansion, which enhanced the government's ability to develop a long-range economic development strategy that created a ripple effect in other sectors of its economy. South Africa again looked to the United States as a market for its raw materials and a supplier of finished goods as in the late nineteenth century.

The resurgence of South African demand for American goods enabled companies such as Johnson and Johnson, Colgate-Palmolive, Coca-Cola, Dun and Bradstreet, Columbia Records, Harley-Davidson, Firestone, Mobil Oil and Standard Oil to deeply penetrate the market. Sales of American goods went from $22 million in 1933 to $89 million in 1937, then skyrocketing to $187 million in 1941.[15] American firms captured nearly 50 percent of non-British exports to South Africa, and by 1938, their investments totaled nearly $80 million.

Washington officials resumed initiatives designed to stimulate American exports by establishing the Reciprocal Trade Agreements Act of 1934 and the Merchant Marine Act of 1936. These measures reinforced the long-term commercial relationship with South Africa that had originated with the National Defense Act of 1920. Although the 1920 act began as a conference to reassess the role of minerals in national defense after World War I,[16] political turmoil in Europe in the late 1930s heightened American fears about potential mineral shortages. Congress responded by passing the National Stockpiling Act of 1939, which enabled the federal government to acquire and store minerals for national defense.

As in the previous world war, opportunities for expanding U.S. trade with South Africa improved with the onset of World War II. As South Africa found itself cut off from traditional supplies in Britain, it came to rely upon American petroleum, aircraft, and private investment dollars. Mutual tourism, a failing prospect before the depression, revived when Pan American Airways launched regular air service from Johannesburg to New York in 1947 and the South African Tourist Corporation opened a New York office in 1949.[17]

Rising tensions between the West and the Soviet bloc after the war made the United States more dependent on strategic minerals. As the Cold War military buildup continued, the Truman administration recognized Pretoria's fervent anticommunism. Yet the relationship created a dilemma because it undermined two fundamental principles—antiimperialism and racial justice—that the United States had endorsed during World War II. South Africa and the other settler-dominated states in southern Africa, as well as Angola, Mozambique, and Southern Rhodesia, quickly suppressed anticolonial protests. The South African government sought to reverse the steady gains made by African workers since the late 1930s. Repressive measures against nonwhites accompanied the growth of Afrikaner nationalism after the National Party gained control of the government in 1948. Afrikaner rule coincided with a new round of anti-American protectionism.

The Truman administration hesitated to criticize the South African government's repressive policies,[18] but several domestic groups rallied to oppose U.S. association with apartheid. The Council on African Affairs, an interracial but black-led organization, was formed in 1937 to support the decolonization of Africa. Its membership included the internationally renowned activist-singer Paul Robeson, Howard University political scientist Ralph Bunche, Harvard anthropologist Raymond Leslie Buell, and Max Yergan, a YMCA official with extensive work experience in South Africa. The New York-based council relied on pressure group and mass mobilization tactics in its efforts to influence American policy. It organized rallies, issued press releases, published a journal called *New Africa*, and lobbied U.S. and UN officials on behalf of black South Africans. In 1950, the council demanded the expulsion of South Africa from the UN.[19]

The rigidity of the Cold War imposed both internal and external constraints on the council's efforts to continue exerting leadership on South African affairs. A major rift emerged within the organization over anticommunism, pitting leftists such as Robeson and William Alphaeus Hunton, a Howard University philosopher, against Yergan, who left the council a short time later. Intimidation and harassment by the FBI and the Department of Justice further weakened the council. Anticommunism took its toll on other black groups in the embryonic Africanist constituency. As the search for radicals and subversives intensified, black activists quickly realized that the Truman administration would use association with the left and criticisms of U.S. policies toward Africa to decimate the ranks of those who supported civil rights at home.[20] Civil rights groups wedded to Truman's Cold War policies unknowingly accelerated the death of the council, which folded in 1955.

Western Cold War containment strategies entailed creating a series of alliances in which member states would pool certain foreign policy objectives in the interest of collective security. One of the first, the North Atlantic Treaty Organization, was concluded in 1949. The original signatories were Belgium, Canada, Denmark, France, Iceland, Italy, Luxembourg, the Netherlands, Norway, Portugal, the United Kingdom, and the United States. Greece and Turkey joined the alliance in 1952, and West Germany signed on in 1955. During the early Cold War period, the anti-Soviet alliance helped justify delaying colonial independence. NATO also furnished an excuse for Portugal to forgo it entirely and provided logistical support for suppressing African nationalist movements. The United States, in its enthusiasm for containing Soviet influence and suppressing radical change, turned a blind eye to Portugal's diversion of NATO weaponry to wars in its colonies.

The Cold War dealt a severe blow to radical efforts to influence both the domestic civil rights movement and the pace of decolonization.[21] A new generation of liberal Africanists nevertheless emerged from the transformation of American missionary societies and the expansion of foundation, corporate, and government involvement in Africa. The elaboration of the apartheid state bureaucracy displaced many of the educational and social services traditionally performed by missionaries. In the United States, missionary ideology came under attack from younger church leaders espousing a form of liberation theology. For many of them, political activism resulted from involvement with the Congress of Racial Equality (CORE) and other pacifist reform groups. The acceleration of the National Party's restrictive legislation—such measures as the Group Areas Act of 1950—commanded significant American liberal attention and led to close monitoring of resistance efforts, especially the Defiance Campaign of 1952. American pacifists initiated correspondences with leaders of the ANC and the South African Indian Congress and through mass mailings and distribution of leaflets urged Americans to oppose segregation abroad as well as at home.[22]

As the Defiance Campaign demonstrated increasing resistance to apartheid, a group called Americans for South African Resistance (AFSAR) organized to provide material support and lobby at the UN. Their first public meeting, held at Reverend Adam Clayton Powell's Abyssinian Baptist Church in Harlem on April 6, 1952, raised nearly $300 to send to the ANC. Less than a year later, this ad hoc group emerged as the American Committee on Africa (ACOA). Its executive committee included George Houser, a staff member of the Fellowship of Reconciliation; James Farmer, who later became director of CORE; socialist Norman Thomas; pacifist A. J. Muste; Roger Baldwin, director of the American Civil Liberties Union; Howard University history professor Rayford Logan; George Carpenter, Africa secretary of the National Council of Churches; and Walter Offutt of the NAACP.[23]

Although ACOA consisted of people active in the civil rights movement, few of them had any direct experience with Africa. The organization's initial efforts revolved around information provision and public education. It sponsored public meetings for African political figures visiting the UN and the United States. However, events steered ACOA toward adopting a more aggressive stance in late 1956, when the South African government arrested a group of moderate anti-apartheid activists and charged them with treason. ACOA responded by establishing the South African Defense Fund to provide legal assistance. ACOA's interest in public education gradually merged with its South African emphasis in 1957, when it launched a major campaign featuring the Declaration of Conscience Against Apartheid. The declaration was a moral appeal to the international community to protest South Africa's racist institutions on Human Rights Day, December 10, 1957.[24] "Freedom and human dignity are in grave jeopardy in the Union of South Africa today," the document emphasized. "The government of that nation continues to extend relentlessly its racist policy of apartheid into the economic, educational, religious and other areas of life."[25] The American signatories of the declaration included Eleanor Roosevelt, Martin Luther King Jr., and labor leader Walter Reuther.

Two other notable Africa-focused organizations appeared during this era. The African-American Institute, initially a Washington, D.C.–based group, was founded in 1952. Its primary activities involved information dissemination and cultural exchange programs for African students and visitors and for domestic audiences with a general interest in Africa. Similarly, the American Society of African Culture (AMSAC), founded in 1956, consisted mainly of black American writers, academics, and artists, involved in the study and dissemination of African culture and heritage. Both organizations had only short-lived existences, as they failed to cultivate a substantial constituency and funding base beyond foundations and corporate donors.[26]

Group formation coincided with growing academic interest in Africa. Major foundations contributed to the expansion and development of African studies programs, beginning in the late 1940s and continuing with support for the nascent African Studies Association in 1957. The development of African studies provided a crucial link for the embryonic anti-apartheid movement. Area studies revitalization, largely funded by philanthropic organizations and government agencies, evolved from a need to address rapid decolonization in Africa and Asia.[27]

Unfortunately, the new groups and academic associations bore the imprint of the Cold War and America's own reluctance to abandon segregation. The new structure of African group representation ironically reproduced segregation on a larger scale. Predominantly black organizations found themselves confined to the cultural arena, frequently outside the academy and without access to political leadership, while Cold War liberals in the embryonic Africanist constituency discouraged civil rights groups from internationalizing their struggle.[28]

Conclusion

The preceding survey suggests that two major axes—the economic benefits that resulted from trade and the political supports required to maintain those arrangements—shaped U.S. policy toward South Africa. The core features of the relationship included American provision of critical services to the expanding South African economy, access to its mineral wealth, and access to its markets. Maintaining the relationship involved assembling a network of American business, finance, and industrial specialists, as well as diplomats and missionaries.[29] The structural features of the relationship produced extraordinary benefits for this narrow range of participants, but its success left them vulnerable to political disruptions inside South Africa. Opponents of white supremacy and missionaries, philanthropists, and civil rights activists questioned the legitimacy of U.S. complicity in the apartheid system.

The imbalance in organizations and structural access is perhaps best illustrated by the monopolization of the politics surrounding U.S. policymaking toward South Africa. The federal government and corporations actively promoted trade at home and abroad, remaining oblivious to South Africa's repressive racial policies. Because the growth of trade enhanced American global power, government officials leaned toward corporate interests in defining and initiating policies toward South Africa. The oppositional sector, by contrast, largely composed of blacks at home and abroad, missionaries, and humanitarian activists, lacked effective organization. It inspired little confidence from either Pretoria or Washington. Quite often, the South African government restricted missionary access to significant portions of the country and severely controlled the entry of black American missionaries and similarly suspect visitors.

The economic power of American businesses involved in South Africa abetted the emergence of the United States as a global power.[30] Profit maximization depended on skills exported to develop key sectors of the South African economy and gain access to its expanding domestic and regional markets. The political and economic vulnerability of blacks and other non-Europeans underwrote the system. The interplay of these factors prevented the formation of any strong opposition to apartheid in the American domestic political arena. Foreign policy critics lacked structural access to the decisionmaking process.

The structural barriers they faced resulted from policymakers' reliance on entrenched networks of political representation and on restrictions on the articulation of antagonistic interests. In this manner, policymaker predilections for defining U.S. interests in particular ways were reinforced. Time-honored and unassailable principles—such as the encouragement of free trade, the Monroe Doctrine principle of nonintervention, and the avoidance of "premature independence" for nonwhite peoples not yet trained in democratic institutions[31]—rationalized the Cold War objective of containing radical change. Without effective opposition, Washington officials treated business interests as identical to the national interest.

Notes

1. John Gaventa, *Power and Powerlessness: Quiescence and Rebellion in an Appalachian Valley* (Urbana: University of Illinois Press, 1980), p. 11; E. E. Schattschneider, *The Semi-Sovereign People: A Realist's View of Democracy in America* (New York: Holt, Rinehart and Winston, 1960), p. 105.

2. Richard W. Hull, *American Enterprise in South Africa: Historical Dimensions of Engagement and Disengagement* (New York: New York University Press, 1990), p. 19; Thomas J. Noer, *Briton, Boer, and Yankee: The United States and South Africa, 1870–1914* (Kent, Ohio: Kent State University Press, 1978), pp. 136–144; Eric Rosenthal, *Stars and Stripes in Africa* (Johannesburg: G. Routledge and Sons, 1968), pp. 121–128.

3. Hull, *American Enterprise*, pp. 67–68.

4. Stuart Anderson, "Racial Anglo-Saxonism and the American Response to the Boer War," *Diplomatic History* 2 (Summer 1978):219–236.

5. Noer, *Briton, Boer, and Yankee*, p. 17.

6. John H. Ferguson, *American Diplomacy and the Boer War* (Philadelphia: University of Pennsylvania Press, 1939), pp. 176–221.

7. Hull, *American Enterprise*, pp. 126–127.

8. Clement Keto, "American Involvement in South Africa, 1870–1915: The Role of Americans in the Creation of Modern South Africa," Ph.D. diss., Georgetown University, 1972.

9. J. Mutero Chirenje, *Ethiopianism and Afro-Americans in Southern Africa, 1883–1916* (Baton Rouge: Louisiana State University Press, 1987).

10. Ibid., pp. 144–162; Noer, *Briton, Boer, and Yankee*, pp. 116–117.

11. Edward Berman, *The Influence of the Carnegie, Ford, and Rockefeller Foundations on American Foreign Policy: The Ideology of Philanthropy* (Albany: SUNY Press, 1983), pp. 22–23; Louis R. Harlan and Raymond W. Smock, eds., *The Booker T. Washington Papers* (Urbana: University of Illinois Press, 1977), pp. 1901–1902.

12. "Opinion," *Crisis* 6 (September 1913):231.

13. Robert A. Hill and Gregory A. Pirio, "'Africa for the Africans': the Garvey Movement in South Africa, 1920–1940," in Shula Marks and Stanley Trapido, eds., *The Politics of Race, Class, and Nationalism in Twentieth-Century South Africa* (New York: Longman, 1987), pp. 209–253.

14. Edward H. Berman, "Educational Colonialism in Africa: The Role of American Foundations, 1910–1945," in Robert F. Arnove, ed., *Philanthropy and Cultural Imperialism: The Foundations at Home and Abroad* (Bloomington: Indiana University Press, 1980), pp. 184–185; Raymond Leslie Buell, *The Native Problem in Africa* (New York: Macmillan, 1928); Franz Boas, *The Mind of Primitive Man* (New York: Macmillan, 1911) and *Race, Language, and Culture* (New York: Macmillan, 1940); Martin Staniland, *American Intellectuals and African Nationalists, 1955–1970* (New Haven: Yale University Press, 1991), pp. 23–24; Peter J. Seybold, "The Ford Foundation and the Triumph of Behavioralism in American Political Science," in Robert F. Arnove, *Philanthropy and Cultural Imperialism*, p. 269.

15. U.S. Department of Commerce, *Statistical Abstracts of the United States, 1930–1985*, nos. 51–106.

16. Stephen Krasner, *Defending the National Interest: Raw Materials Investments and U.S. Foreign Policy* (Princeton: Princeton University Press, 1978).

17. Hull, *American Enterprise*, p. 221.

18. Thomas Borstelman, *Apartheid's Reluctant Uncle: The United States and Southern Africa in the Early Cold War* (New York: Oxford University Press, 1993).

19. Hollis R. Lynch, *Black American Radicals and the Liberation of Africa: The Council on African Affairs, 1937–1955* (Ithaca: Cornell University Africana Studies and Research Center, 1978).

20. James Roark, "American Black Leaders: The Response to Colonialism and the Cold War, 1943–1953," *African Historical Studies* 4 (1971):253–270.

21. Mark Solomon, "Black Critics," in Thomas Paterson, ed., *Cold War Critics: Alternatives to American Foreign Policy in the Truman Years* (Chicago: Quadrangle Books, 1971); Gerald Horne, *Black and Red: W.E.B. Du Bois and the Afro-American Response to the Cold War, 1944–1963* (Albany: SUNY Press, 1986).

22. George Houser, *No One Can Stop the Rain: Glimpses of Africa's Liberation Struggle* (New York: Pilgrim Press, 1989), p. 14.

23. Ibid., p. 63.

24. George M. Houser, "Meeting Africa's Challenge: The Story of the American Committee on Africa," *Issue: A Quarterly Journal of Africanist Opinion* 6, 2–3 (Summer–Fall 1976):16–26.

25. Houser, *No One Can Stop the Rain*, p. 123.

26. Francis E. Kornegay Jr., "Black American and U.S.–Southern African Relations: An Essay Bibliographical Survey of Developments During the 1950s, 1960s, and Early 1970s," in Mohamed A. El-Khawas and Francis E. Kornegay Jr., eds., *American-Southern African Relations: Bibliographic Essays* (Westport, Conn.: Greenwood Press, 1975), pp. 144–147.

27. Berman, *Influence of the Carnegie, Ford, and Rockefeller Foundations*.

28. Elliott P. Skinner, "Afro-Americans in Search of Africa: The Scholars," in Pearl T. Robinson and Elliott P. Skinner, eds., *Transformation and Resiliency in Africa: As Seen by Afro-American Scholars* (Washington, D.C.: Howard University Press, 1983), pp. 17–24.

29. Emily Rosenberg, *Spreading the American Dream: American Economic and Cultural Expansion, 1890–1945* (New York: Hill and Wang, 1982).

30. William Minter, *King Solomon's Mines Revisited: Western Interests and the Burdened History of Southern Africa* (New York: Basic Books, 1986).

31. Henry Byroade, "The World's Colonies and Ex-Colonies: A Challenge to America," *State Department Bulletin* 29 (November 16, 1953):655–660.

3

The Sharpeville Massacre and the Rise of U.S. Anti-Apartheid Activism, 1960–1968

Studies of U.S. policy toward South Africa often refer to the Sharpeville massacre as the crisis moment that brought apartheid to the attention of the American public and served as a catalyst for the anti-apartheid movement.[1] Although crisis events provide opportunities to voice criticisms of established policies, seldom do those moments furnish sufficient resources and momentum to sustain protest. Consistent with the revised political process model, this chapter examines how a set of entrenched international power relationships, shaken by reactions to the Sharpeville massacre, evolved into a series of strategies to contain external criticism of apartheid, increases in South African controls on black labor mobility and political activity, and isolated American liberal opposition. Although these developments narrowed the political opportunity structure for anti-apartheid activism, they compelled foreign policy critics to intensify their analysis of the internal and external power arrangements that reinforced South Africa's system of racial inequality. Subsequent reevaluations of movement strategies and organizational structure by activists led to a gradual shift from reactive to active protest modes.

The Structure of Political Opportunity

The year 1960 stirred rising hopes for political change throughout Africa. The UN admitted seventeen new African states and designated 1960 "The Year of Africa." Proponents of racial justice worldwide expected that the momentum of decolonization would leave no region of Africa unchanged. Anxiety over race relations accompanied the intensifying domestic civil rights movement, then in its direct action phase. Democratic presidential candidate John F. Kennedy campaigned on Dwight D. Eisenhower's failure to abandon a colonial view of Africa.[2] Converging racial crises at home and abroad enlarged political space on two fronts for critics of administration policy.

Eisenhower responded to criticisms by altering the appearance rather than the substance of his African policy. The administration sent a high-profile delegation to Ghana's independence celebrations in March 1957, and the following year, the State Department established the Bureau of African Affairs. These bureaucratic responses could not conceal a perfunctory commitment to racial equality and self-determination in Africa and a willingness to excuse apartheid because of South Africa's unwavering anticommunism. The administration defended South Africa at home and at the United Nations, concluded a nuclear cooperation agreement with South Africa to expand the uses of atomic energy, and entered into a mutual defense compact that provided for three satellite tracking stations and joint naval exercises. Adherence to Cold War doctrines rationalized a "middle-road" strategy that acknowledged the right of colonized peoples to self-determination but warned against "premature independence" that could undermine European and South African interests.[3]

Beginning with its 1948 electoral victory, South Africa's National Party government took advantage of the veneer of legitimacy afforded by its ideological, strategic, and economic relationships with Western powers to extend its mission of separate racial development and institutionalize it within the framework of an expanding industrial economy. Throughout the 1950s, the state pursued a comprehensive system of laws and regulations to secure white supremacy, solidify racial segregation, control the movement of black labor, and suppress emergent black political activity. The National Party articulation of the apartheid system, however, led to the protests that exposed Pretoria to international criticism and accelerated the drive for black political power.

Labor conflicts furnished much of the impetus for the wave of protest that arose during the first decade of the apartheid system. By the late 1950s, the fiercest resistance was leveled against state attempts to control and restrict black physical mobility. Two particular policies—the forced removal of blacks from urban areas and the implementation of a pass law system—especially provoked African wrath. Black political mobilization nevertheless remained fragmented. The two major groups, the Pan-African Congress (PAC) and the African National Congress, pursued distinct ideologies and constituencies. The ANC included Africans, Coloureds, Indians, and whites, whereas the nationalist PAC remained suspicious of non-African commitment to resistance efforts.[4] Ironically, division between the two ignited the state's most severe early crisis.

In December 1959, both the ANC and the PAC announced plans for a national anti–pass law campaign. The PAC, which had split off from the

ANC a year earlier, set March 21, 1960, as the date for launching its campaign. On that day, a crowd of more than 5,000 gathered to peacefully demonstrate at a police station in the black township of Sharpeville, about thirty miles south of Johannesburg. The protest took an unexpected turn when police opened fire on the crowd, killing sixty-nine and wounding nearly 200.

The events at Sharpeville touched off a series of nationwide protests. The ANC, which had planned its pass law protest for March 31, called for a work stoppage on March 28. In major cities around the country, an overwhelming majority of African workers refused to report for work. On March 30, a spontaneous demonstration at the Houses of Parliament drew more than 30,000. Despite more than two weeks of protest following the massacre, the state remained firmly in control, temporarily suspending pass law enforcement to concentrate on destroying the resistance movement. On April 8, the state banned the PAC and ANC, and during the next six weeks, police arrested more than 18,000 people.[5] Sharpeville had a profound affect on the course of anti-apartheid resistance, as it simultaneously forced activists to reconsider their strategies and extended international awareness of their struggle.

Images of the massacre, carried by the international media, provoked anger and spontaneous demonstrations at South African embassies and consulates around the world. The UN General Assembly, replete with new African and Asian member states eager to alter the agenda of the international community, sent a clear message to South Africa when it resolved that all states "consider taking such separate and collective action as is open to them under the UN Charter to bring about the abandonment of apartheid policies."[6] The resolution marked the first time that the UN urged member states to take action against apartheid. Over the next three years, the General Assembly made several attempts to persuade member states to move against South Africa. In 1962, a resolution calling for economic and diplomatic sanctions as well as an arms embargo passed by a vote of 67 to 16, with 23 abstentions. Although not binding on member states, this resolution facilitated a partial embargo on weapons sales to Pretoria in 1964.

The State Department immediately condemned the violence at Sharpeville but encouraged Africans to maintain a commitment to nonviolent protest. Washington officials nevertheless considered the incident an internal South African matter and urged restraint upon the international community. Their response created a major bureaucratic rift and demonstrated the Eisenhower administration's sensitivity to the white South African viewpoint. The administration disciplined Public Affairs Officer Lincoln White for declaring that the United States "condemns violence in all forms" and supports the right "of all African people in South

Africa . . . to obtain redress for legitimate grievances by peaceful means."
The president quickly distanced himself from White's remarks, characterizing apartheid as a "touchy thing" and insisting that critics consider
the needs of a valued ally. Eisenhower's reactions revealed less concern
with the injustices of apartheid than with the difficulties of explaining the
close relationship with a government so openly contemptuous of its
black citizens. The administration felt that any public acknowledgment
of the legitimacy of black protest might lead South Africa to curtail
American access to strategic minerals or close its ports to U.S. fleets.[7]

Strong reactions to the bloody events at Sharpeville did not make
Americans any more familiar with Africa, and there was little news beyond crisis-oriented reportage to fill the informational void. The out-
break of civil war in the Congo in June 1960 added to their confusion.
Like Sharpeville, the Congo crisis drew substantial media coverage. For
the impressionable U.S. public, however, the imagery of retaliatory violence against whites, "tribalism," and Soviet penetration reinforced the
idea that premature African independence was highly dangerous.[8]

Sharpeville posed an immediate threat to one of the world's fastest-
growing economies, since it shook the confidence of both the South
African business community and foreign investors. The crisis coincided
with a period of comparative economic stagnation that resulted from increased labor unrest and uncertainty over the country's political direction in the wake of the decolonization momentum. International investment capital, which had consistently played a major role in South
Africa's development, withdrew nearly $200 million by the end of 1960
(Figure 3.1).[9]

South African business associations publicly acknowledged Sharpeville as a product of the legitimate grievances of African laborers and
called for immediate government reforms to ease racial tensions. Co-
optative rather than conciliatory business recommendations included relaxation of labor mobility and pass laws for Africans already living in
urban areas but insisted on maintaining the distinction between urban
and migrant Africans.[10]

Although hesitant at the earliest stage of the crisis, U.S. businesses
began to regain confidence in South Africa by early 1961. Much of the initiative for revitalizing American investments came from Charles W.
Engelhard, the largest single U.S. investor in South Africa. Engelhard
controlled more than twenty major enterprises in South Africa, including
key operations in gold and uranium mining. As a result of his leadership,
a group of American financiers assembled a $150 million loan for the
troubled South African government from a combination of sources, including Chase Manhattan Bank, First National City Bank, the International Monetary Fund (IMF), and the World Bank. The loan materialized

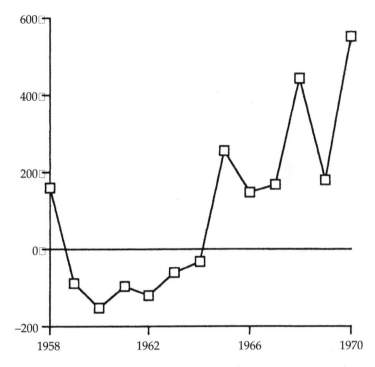

FIGURE 3.1   Net Flow of Foreign Capital to South Africa, 1958–1970 (in millions of rands)

SOURCE: South African Reserve Bank, *Quarterly Bulletin, no. 97*, September 1970.

at a critical time, furnishing capital to revitalize the economy and rein-forcing the apartheid system's security orientation by assisting industries in the state-controlled sector.[11]

Engelhard's pivotal role illustrates South Africa's structural access to American entrepreneurs and public-sector policymakers and reveals a major obstacle confronting anti-apartheid activists. Apart from his ties to international finance, Engelhard commanded the respect of liberal busi-ness leaders. He had received several awards for his support for civil rights. Engelhard contributed generously to the Democratic Party and maintained a close friendship with then vice president, later president, Lyndon Johnson. A racial liberal at home, Johnson supported and bene-fited from racial oppression abroad.[12]

Anglo-American Corporation of South Africa, like Englehard himself, provided another critical link to U.S. capital. Founded in 1917 to exploit opportunities in South African gold mining, Anglo-American derived nearly half of its initial capital from North American sources. South

African industrialist Ernest Oppenheimer bought out most of the American interest in the corporation during the late 1920s, but it remained one of the principal mechanisms for channeling U.S. capital into South Africa's extractive industries. Working with Englehard and other foreign investors, Anglo-American took advantage of the post-Sharpeville financial crisis to strengthen its position in mining and combine its interests with the strategic needs of the South African state, especially its defense establishment.[13]

Companies such as Ford and General Motors kept their South African investments, while Firestone, Dow Chemical, and Kaiser Aluminum established new operations. Direct U.S. investment increased by $23 million in 1961, rising to $44 million in 1962. American investors concentrated on the sectors of South Africa's economy that related directly to industrialization and militarization, including transportation, petroleum products, and computer technology. U.S. corporations played a significant role in providing the technological and managerial assistance that South Africa needed to attain self-sufficiency and withstand international opposition.[14]

South Africa had recuperated by 1964 from the stagnation induced by earlier political uncertainties. International capital had underwritten the restructuring necessary to reinforcing the state's commitment to apartheid. Through bureaucratic expansion and centralization, state intervention in the economy touched ever more areas: planning, investment, infrastructure development, labor control, and regulation of capital mobility. South Africa thereafter joined Japan as the world's fastest-growing economy during the latter half of the 1960s.[15]

Economic revitalization relied heavily upon the political and bureaucratic domination of the black population. The state continually fine-tuned its security apparatus to maintain rigid control over black labor organizations and black demographic movement. The extended policy reach of security agencies, such as the Department of Bantu Administration and Development (BAD), reinforced an elaborate physical and social control infrastructure. It included a technologically advanced arrest, detention, prison, and execution system; laws mandating separation of black urban workers from their families; revocation of South African citizenship for surplus black workers; refinement of the racial classification system; an extensive system of private shooting clubs for the putative self-defense of whites; use of multiracial teams to infiltrate opposition groups; and purging of white liberals from state employment.[16] By the mid-1960s, the state had effectively crushed domestic opposition, arrested dissident leaders, and driven much of the protest movement underground or into exile.

As part of the strategy to improve its reputation abroad, South Africa embarked upon an ideological offensive in the United States. In June

1960, South African ambassador Wentzel C. du Plessis explained in a *U.S. News and World Report* article that his nation's discrimination policies remained within the range of practices common in other societies. Pretoria tried to reassure the American business community and gain more access to policymaking circles by hiring a New York public relations firm, the Hamilton Wright Organization, to create a favorable image of South Africa. Later that year, the semiofficial South African Foundation established offices in New York City and Washington, D.C., to promote South Africa as an attractive site for foreign investments.[17]

South African officials not only feared African nationalist challenges to minority rule but also worried that African-American activism might influence U.S. foreign policy. Historian Thomas Noer contends that "South Africans were interested in the battles in Mississippi, Alabama, and the rest of the South. Even though they feared the rise in black militancy in the United States, they also tried to use it as proof of the need for strict white control. Verwoerd cited the violence in America in a speech to parliament defending racial separatism and white political dominance."[18]

Eisenhower had remained impervious to the turmoil surrounding the Sharpeville massacre, but the election of John F. Kennedy in November 1960 heightened expectations that the United States would exert greater pressure on South Africa. Optimism grew out of campaign rhetoric and extended into Kennedy's filling key appointments with liberals who either had experience in Africa or had ties to domestic civil rights constituencies. They included: Adlai Stevenson, the Democratic presidential candidate in 1952 and 1956, as ambassador to the UN; former Michigan governor G. Mennen Williams, who had been ambassador to India, as assistant secretary of state for African affairs; Chester Bowles as undersecretary of State; and Ford Foundation executive J. Wayne Fredericks as Williams's deputy secretary. During Kennedy's first year in office, Williams and Stevenson demonstrated in their public speeches and policy pronouncements a willingness to break the official silence on apartheid.

Liberal initiatives, however, could not overcome entrenched opposition from veteran cold warriors who asserted the priority of national security concerns as justification for maintaining the status quo in South African–American relations. Secretary of State Dean Rusk and Joseph Satterthwaite, ambassador to South Africa, adamantly rejected any consideration of economic sanctions as a policy option. The Defense Department in December 1961 concluded an agreement to establish missile range-tracking facilities in South Africa. In exchange for access to those facilities, the administration agreed to sell military equipment to South Africa for exclusive use against "external" rather than internal opponents of apartheid.[19]

Perhaps the best illustration of the depth of U.S. commitment to Pretoria was the work of the Central Intelligence Agency. After South Africa withdrew from the British Commonwealth in 1961, the CIA assumed a larger role in the coordination and training of Pretoria's intelligence services. Impressed with South African anticommunism, the CIA enthusiastically assisted the government's campaign of infiltration and destruction of liberal, as well as radical, opposition groups. The agency played a significant role in the August 1962 capture of ANC underground leader Nelson Mandela.[20]

Kennedy and his successor, Lyndon B. Johnson, attempted a dual strategy of appeasing the domestic civil rights constituency and African leaders with sharp criticism of apartheid. At the same time, they continued the extensive ties to South Africa. Although initially effective, this approach created a set of interlocking relationships between domestic and foreign policy that simultaneously rendered race-relations problems more visible and hindered their solution. For example, Johnson marshaled legislative forces in early 1964 to secure passage of the Civil Rights Act and strengthen his bid to become the Democratic Party's presidential candidate. He used the legislative victory to fortify his domestic coalition and as a tool to maintain credibility among the Afro-Asian diplomatic communities at the UN and in Washington.[21] Yet preserving trustworthiness demanded reciprocal policy initiatives. The absence of such advances contributed to the gradual dissolution of the administration's domestic and international coalitions.

Throughout the 1960s, the web of interests linking Pretoria and Washington furnished a series of crisis opportunities for American policymakers. In August 1963, the United States supported a UN resolution that called for a ban on weapons sales to South Africa. Lobbying and delay by the U.S. mission produced an arms embargo with significant symbolic value but imposed few constraints on American and other suppliers to South Africa. The Johnson administration sent former solicitor general Judge Charles Fahy to officially observe the trial of Mandela and nine others in spring 1964. After a South African court found five of the defendants guilty and sentenced them to life imprisonment, Fahy concluded that the proceedings had been fair and that the defendants were guilty of revolutionary activity.[22]

Another controversy erupted in February 1967, when the USS *FDR*, returning from service in Vietnam, docked at Capetown. American and South African officials developed plans for entertaining the interracial crew, but Pretoria abruptly announced its intention to enforce segregation laws. After its brief stop, during which the South Africans slightly moderated the ban on interracial shore leaves, U.S. naval officials ordered the *FDR* home.

Other events in the mid-1960s demonstrated a similar U.S. reluctance to be forthright on international questions having to do with race and colonialism. These include American military involvement in the 1964 rescue of Belgian settlers in the Congo and Portugal's use of U.S.-supplied NATO weapons in its war against Angolan nationalists. Each of these events gave the United States a chance to support its rhetorical commitment to decolonization. Instead, by avoidance and deflection, Washington policymakers acknowledged their unwillingness to undermine colonial and neocolonial priorities.[23]

The political opportunity structure for mobilizing opposition to lenient South African policies steadily diminished during Johnson's second term. It did so in an environment that suggested strong parallels between domestic and foreign policy objectives in addressing racial conflict. These occasionally emerged in public discourse, but Cold War priorities kept these areas distinct and invisible to all but the most determined observers. The national movement for racial equality, for example, faced new obstacles, including federal ambivalence, when U.S. activists shifted their focus to Northern cities. In Africa, as the decolonization movement gravitated southward to territories more strategically and economically central to Cold War constructions of the national interest, U.S. policymakers developed more elaborate rationales for procrastination on the independence question.

Organizational Developments

The political uncertainty surrounding the Sharpeville massacre touched off minor debates among policymakers that outwardly presented a favorable climate for organizing American opposition to apartheid. Yet the movement did not unfold in a linear pattern of membership recruitment, strategy development, and group coordination, as suggested by organizationally based explanations such as resource mobilization. This is partially explained by the character of foreign policymaking, which traditionally excludes citizen or nonelite group participation and by American society's ambivalence toward race and Africa. The absence of a clear target to channel oppositional energy drove the earliest stage of anti-apartheid activism into exploration of new political spaces, practices, and organizational forms. This search for appropriate venues, tactics, and resources constituted a highly politicized process that shaped subsequent movement development, as competing agendas emerged among activist factions and within the secluded state-sanctioned policymaking sphere.[24]

Monitoring of South African race relations during the 1952 Defiance Campaign led a coalition of nonviolent social activists to form an ad hoc group, Americans for South African Resistance (AFSAR). The next year AFSAR evolved into the American Committee on Africa, a permanent, generally focused organization that served as a major source of information and public education on Africa. ACOA nevertheless played a critical role in connecting pacifists, labor unions, and civil rights groups to the international struggle against apartheid.

ACOA and other Africa-focused groups in the pre-Sharpeville era operated as information clearing houses rather than as political action groups. They eschewed the militant anticolonialism that would raise Cold War hackles. Although interracial membership was common, most organizations maintained few ties to indigenous institutions within the African-American community that had served as major catalysts for civil rights activism. The most directly engaged group action by Americans against apartheid occurred in 1957, when a delegation from the Southern Christian Leadership Conference (SCLC), buoyed by the successful bus boycott in Montgomery, Alabama, traveled to Alexandra, South Africa, to help build a similar movement.[25] This transnational effort achieved limited success in South Africa but produced no ripple effect in the United States.

The American Committee on Africa took the initiative in coordinating anti-apartheid activities in the immediate aftermath of Sharpeville. Just two days after the March 21 incident, ACOA and the Congress of Racial Equality organized a New York City march to a Woolworth's department store and then on to the South African consulate. These actions symbolically linked the Southern-based direct action movement with opposition to apartheid. On April 13, ACOA launched the Emergency South Africa Campaign to provide education about apartheid, raise funds, and encourage boycotts of South African–produced consumer goods and U.S. businesses that supported apartheid.[26]

ACOA initiatives also sought to strengthen the relationship between civil rights organizations and the Africa support community. With ACOA's encouragement, the American Negro Leadership Conference on Africa (ANLCA) was founded in 1961. It included representatives from six major civil rights organizations: the NAACP, CORE, the National Urban League, the National Council of Negro Women, the SCLC, and the Brotherhood of Sleeping Car Porters. Theodore Brown, a veteran staffer of the last group, served as executive director.[27] Despite efforts to link the two struggles, the ANLCA, an elite group, never cultivated the membership and resource base that would enable it to evolve beyond a mere rhetorical response to crises in American–South African relations. It had folded by 1967.

Other groups linked their struggles to the anti-apartheid movement in spite of the ANLCA's failure. In March 1965, pickets led by the Students for a Democratic Society (SDS) and the National Student Christian Federation demonstrated at the Wall Street headquarters of Chase Manhattan Bank to demand cancellation of its loans to South Africa. SDS organized demonstrations against other banks and corporations involved in South Africa in Boston, Washington, Detroit, and San Francisco. Later that month, the Student Nonviolent Coordinating Committee (SNCC) staged a sit-in at the South African embassy in Washington. In July, the CORE joined SNCC to picket the New York office of the U.S. ambassador to the UN. Protesters demanded that Washington apply economic sanctions and terminate its diplomatic relations with Pretoria.[28]

Still other groups began to organize against apartheid. The United Church of Christ issued a call for sanctions in 1963. More extensive church mobilization developed three years later, when the National Council of Churches began an informational campaign for members about economic ties to apartheid and also encouraged review of church investments in corporations involved in South Africa.[29] The Lawyers Committee for Civil Rights Under Law, created in 1963 by a group of prominent Washington attorneys to challenge racial discrimination in the courts, established the Southern Africa Project in 1967. Project lawyers represented South Africans applying for political asylum and used the law to bar corporations from honoring South African statutes in the conduct of business. The Lawyers Committee initially focused on assisting lawyers in South Africa and Namibia but gradually turned to federal law as an instrument for extending UN antiracist measures.[30]

Selection of protest targets constituted a significant challenge. George Houser, ACOA's executive director, explained how that organization first embraced but then quickly abandoned boycotts of South African-produced goods as the most appropriate target.

> It started for us because there were very few things that we could do; we looked for things that we could boycott but there was very little coming in from South Africa to the United States. Lobster tails—one of the key things—we did a research job on lobster tails to see if that was a campaign, a boycott of lobster tails from South Africa that would catch hold. We came to the conclusion that no, it was not. In Britain, we were closely in touch with the anti-apartheid movement in London—they had boycott campaigns going on.[31]

The pursuit of a focus for channeling movement energies eventually yielded a somewhat novel yet potentially potent strategy: encouraging individuals and organizations to withdraw their funds from banks lending money to South Africa. "There were very few goods being imported into the United States from South Africa that we could boycott,"

Houser recalled. "But there were banks involved and our whole effort began with Chase Manhattan Bank and what was then the First National City Bank, now Citibank, because those were the two banks in the United States that had branches in South Africa."[32]

The political climate of the 1960s broadened public awareness of racial problems in Africa and generated sporadic involvement by groups. The new environment also produced uncertainties about the direction of these energies and thus provoked ACOA, one of the leaders of the fledging Africanist constituency, to reevaluate its organizational structure and mission.[33] According to Houser:

> It was not easy for ACOA to work on these issues effectively. American interest in Africa was not great. Activists were concentrating on the civil rights struggle and the war in Vietnam. Furthermore, an unwarranted feeling of optimism about progress in South Africa pervaded the consciousness of many people, despite Sharpeville. The perception was that things were rapidly changing in Africa; with the birth of so many independent states, the white-dominated governments of Rhodesia, the Portuguese colonies, and South Africa would have to recognize the signs of the times. Only later in the 1960s, as oppression increased in South Africa and guerrilla fighting expanded elsewhere, was the reality of a long-drawn-out struggle recognized.[34]

Recognition of the challenges confronting ACOA within the national structure of group representation also prompted reappraisal. Between the 1953 founding of ACOA and the end of the first wave of African independence movements in the early 1960s, groups like the American Society of African Culture, the African American Institute, Operation Crossroads Africa, the American Southern Africa Council, and the Liberty Lobby claimed to represent indigenous African opinion.[35] ACOA consequently shared its original mission of providing information about Africa with other private-sector organizations, Africa programs of federal agencies, and the news media. ACOA board members recognized that having significant political impact required not only extension of anti-apartheid activities beyond the UN and New York City and the creation of a lobbying apparatus[36] but also incorporation of a broader range of citizens in protest activity.

Like most social movement organizations, ACOA faced ongoing pressures to reexamine its structure and composition. Although the group included black American public figures such as baseball pioneer Jackie Robinson, labor activist A. Philip Randolph, civil rights leaders Martin Luther King Jr., James Farmer, Percy Sutton, and Bayard Rustin, by late 1961 Houser and other key staffers felt that ACOA needed a stronger presence in the black community.[37] The proposal gained considerable support, but no consensus emerged on how to implement it. Initial debate led to the convening of a 1962 conference that resulted in the formation of ANLCA. That organization, and those successfully created by black students in the South, inspired activists to explore new forms of grassroots mobilization.

More comprehensive approaches to expanding ACOA's relationship with the black community and with students did not develop until 1968. At its January meeting, the Executive Board outlined a proposal to sponsor local organizations under ACOA auspices. The plan included three central components:

1. The rising interests in opposition to apartheid in black communities and in middle class white communities warrants the creation of field staffs of organizers who would accelerate the effort to exert pressure on members of Congress, local companies and banks, and public education institutions with ties to South Africa.

2. The social and political activism of the 1960s produced a cadre of young people with experience in organizing, knowledge of African affairs, and able to work for modest salaries (returned Peace Corps volunteers, returned missionaries and clergy, older student movement organizers, and antiwar organizers).

3. The selection of cities for locating the field organization would be: a) communities with sufficient resources for political action(e.g., a large black population, a liberal and articulate clergy, etc.), and b) locally accessible targets for action (city with a member of Congress on the House Subcommittee on Africa, a South Africa consulate, or an industry with major investments in South Africa).[38]

The ACOA staff quickly pursued these new opportunities. In the fall, ACOA began an information, education, and mobilization program in the black Bedford-Stuyvesant section of Brooklyn, New York. The project's first local field worker, Blyden Jackson, had worked with the Student Non-Violent Coordinating Committee.[39] Other elements of ACOA's transition gradually surfaced. Staff members prepared a list of questions for candidates in the presidential primaries. Later that summer, they developed a position paper on South African–American relations to circulate at the Democratic National Convention in Chicago. ACOA lobbied intensively with a committee of top U.S. professional and college athletes and the London-based South Africa Non-Racial Olympic Committee

(SANROC) to exclude South Africa from the 1968 Olympics in Mexico City. Although the U.S. Olympic Committee supported inviting South Africa to the games, the International Olympic Committee voted to maintain its current suspension.[40] By the end of the decade, ACOA had abandoned information dissemination as its principal focus in favor of a more forthrightly political and engaged posture.

The transitions experienced by organizations involved in the anti-apartheid struggle reflected the complex political realities resulting from domestic involvement in the international community and early manifestations of the socioeconomic structural changes associated with postindustrialization.[41] The movement initially relied on traditional bases of support such as the big six civil rights organizations, the Amalgamated Clothing Workers Union, Americans for Democratic Action (ADA), the American Society of African Culture, the International Ladies Garment Workers Union, the Jewish Labor Committee, the AFL-CIO, and the United Auto Workers. During the latter part of the decade, it increasingly drew upon groups representing students, the middle class, academics, lawyers, and other professionals from these growth sectors of American society. This expanded constituency consisted primarily of groups structurally predisposed to define their well-being as compatible with a more diversified international community.[42]

Consciousness-Raising

Anti-apartheid activists witnessed little concrete improvement in the prospects for meaningfully influencing South African–American relations during most of the 1960s. A careful reading of several sources suggests three explanations. First, ethnocentric and racist assumptions about Pretoria's importance to national security limited the extent to which public- and private-sector policymakers would consider alternatives. Second, the South African government and its support network capitalized on the cushion provided by anticommunism with an ideological offensive that further insulated policymaking institutions from oppositional issues and discourses. Third, the development of such political crises in Africa throughout the decade as the overthrow of Kwame Nkrumah of Ghana and the Nigerian civil war seemed to reinforce comfortable doubts about African capacity for self-rule. These emergencies, coupled with widespread public and official ignorance alike, further inhibited debate and strengthened stereotypes that rationalized Cold War perspectives. Africa existed in what Martin Staniland refers to as "a state of conceptual dependency on regions and preoccupations that are closer to the mainstream of American foreign policy." As a result, the policy narratives that interpreted the relationship of African crises to the

United States offered containment of African unrest as the only viable response.[43]

Anti-apartheid activism faced the dual challenge of intervening in public and private policymaking processes and enlarging the constituency to support those endeavors. ACOA recognized the need to develop stronger relations with the black community and student groups, but comprehensive plans for incorporating these new perspectives into the anti-apartheid struggle did not emerge until near the end of the decade, when the political opportunity structure had diminished considerably. With an enlarged network, activists gained access to rank-and-file constituencies in the civil rights, student, and antiwar movements that had developed effective counternarratives to domestic and foreign policy orthodoxy. This expanded constituency was not unaccompanied by conflict, however, as many liberals and church groups, previously sympathetic to African liberation, reconsidered their commitments when black "militants" and student radicals pursued strategies that were more aggressive than they were prepared to endorse.[44] It is ironic that the prospects for anti-apartheid mobilization begin to improve only after 1960s radicalism began exhibiting signs of decay.

Conclusion

The Sharpeville massacre represented one of the most significant actionable issues,[45] or crisis situations, that forced policymakers to defend or explain their response (or nonresponse) in the early postwar era of U.S.–South African relations. It coincided with a period of growing domestic racial tensions and intensification of Cold War competition for the allegiance of the newly independent African states. The U.S. government, in quickly denouncing the shootings at Sharpeville, expressed opposition to racial separation abroad, as well as at home.[46] Despite immediate international reaction to Sharpeville and the rise of other actionable issues around apartheid in the mid-1960s, the crises of this period failed to generate and sustain higher levels of anti-apartheid activism.

The ACOA devoted considerable time and resources to mobilizing around apartheid. It provided a set of focal issues—the symmetry between South African apartheid and American racial segregation, the urgent need to dismantle both, and the imperative that the United States promote itself abroad as a humanitarian force for change. Its specific tactics—marches, demonstrations, relief drives, and conferences—sought to generate a mass movement. Yet ACOA remained primarily New York–based, with very weak links to established political institutions outside that city. During its early years, ACOA considered itself an information clearinghouse rather than a policy advocacy force.[47] ACOA maintained strong ties with liberal groups such as the NAACP, CORE, the Fellowship of Reconciliation, the Congress of Industrial Organizations, and Americans for Democratic Action, but it proved incapable of cultivating two potentially mobilizable populations: black communities and college students. Strengthening such ties required bottom-up rather than top-down strategies. The civil rights movement represented an important alliance and provided a tactical organizational repertory, but it also competed with anti-apartheid groups for scarce resources, members, and political space. A popular anti-apartheid constituency did not emerge until the end of the decade. Activism had extended its reach but lacked the means to sustain its drive.

The Sharpeville crisis and federal and corporate complicity in the maintenance of apartheid presented critical moments for the opposition, yet many of the claims raised by anti-apartheid groups lacked credibility with many Americans. The United States, like South Africa, has a long history of racial segregation, but little else in the national experience up to that time prepared citizens to understand and respond more fully to the apartheid issue. Direct governmental experience with Africa remained limited or covert, and although a number of home-based corporations had extensive South African ties,[48] those connections existed in an informational vacuum.

Maintaining the attractiveness of South Africa as a site for U.S. capital required a public relations apparatus that celebrated profitability while overlooking black suffering. The absence of continuous media coverage contributed to the sense of South Africa as a distant and remote place, and the first generation of critical Africanist scholars had yet to emerge.[49] The Cold War climate, the structural imbalance in access to the policy-making process, and public apathy and indifference toward African liberation underwrote Washington's unwillingness to act decisively. These domestic characteristics, combined with increased political repression in South Africa, severely undermined the political opportunity structure for anti-apartheid activism.

Notes

1. Peter J. Schraeder, *United States Foreign Policy Toward Africa: Incrementalism, Crisis, and Change* (New York: Cambridge University Press, 1994), p. 198.

2. John Mahoney, *JFK: Ordeal in Africa* (New York: Oxford University Press, 1983).

3. Richard W. Hull, *American Enterprise in South Africa: Historical Dimensions of Engagement and Disengagement* (New York: New York University Press, 1990), p. 216; Henry Byroade, "The World's Colonies and Ex-Colonies: A Challenge to America," *State Department Bulletin* 29 (November 16, 1953):655–660.

4. Deborah Posel, *The Making of Apartheid, 1948–1961: Conflict and Compromise* (New York: Clarendon Press, 1991), p. 237; Tom Lodge, *Black Politics in South Africa Since 1945* (New York: Longman, 1983), pp. 84–86.

5. Ibid., pp. 201–226.

6. Resolution 134 (1960): "Question Relating to the Situation in the Union of South Africa," April 1, 1960, in UN Security Council, *Resolutions, 1960* (New York: United Nations, 1960), pp. 1–2.

7. Study Commission on U.S. Policy Toward Southern Africa, *South Africa: Time Running Out* (Berkeley and Los Angeles: University of California Press, 1986), p. 346; Dana Adams Schmidt, "Political Violence in South Africa Criticized by U.S.," *New York Times*, March 23, 1960; "Transcripts of Eisenhower's News Conference on Foreign and Domestic Issues," *New York Times*, March 31, 1960; Thomas J. Noer, *Cold War and Black Liberation: The United States and White Rule in Africa, 1948–1968* (Columbia: University of Missouri Press, 1985), p. 55.

8. Martin Staniland, *American Intellectuals and African Nationalists, 1955–1970* (New Haven: Yale University Press, 1991), pp. 49–52; Stephen F. Weissman, *American Foreign Policy in the Congo, 1960–1964* (Ithaca: Cornell University Press, 1974); F. Chidozie Ogene, *Interest Groups and the Shaping of Foreign Policy* (New York: St. Martin's Press, 1983), pp. 24–25.

9. David Pallister, Sarah Stewart, and Ian Lepper, *South Africa, Inc.: The Oppenheimer Empire* (New Haven: Yale University Press, 1987), p. 95.

10. Posel, *The Making of Apartheid*, p. 239.

11. Barbara Rogers, *White Wealth and Black Poverty* (Westport, Conn.: Greenwood Press, 1976), pp. 102–103; Ann Seidman, *The Roots of Crisis in Southern Africa* (Trenton, N.J.: Africa World Press, 1985), pp. 43–47.

12. "The Engelhard Touch," *Forbes* 96 (August 1, 1965), pp. 20–25.

13. Duncan Innes, *Anglo-American and the Rise of Modern South Africa* (New York: Monthly Review Press, 1984), p. 92; Pallister, Stewart, and Lepper, *South Africa, Inc.*, p. 29.

14. Ogene, *Interest Groups*, p. 158; Seidman, *The Roots of Crisis*, p. 47.

15. Posel, *The Making of Apartheid*, pp. 256–267; William Minter, *King Solomon's Mines Revisited: Western Interests and the Burdened History of Southern Africa* (New York: Basic Books, 1986), p. 213.

16. Noer, *Cold War and Black Liberation*, p. 130.

17. Wentzel C. du Plessis, "Apartheid: Is it Really Race Discrimination?" *U.S. News and World Report* 48, 25 (June 20, 1960), pp. 138–139; U.S. Congress, Senate, Committee on Foreign Relations, *Activities on Non-Diplomatic Representatives of Foreign Principles in the United States, Hearings before the Committee on Foreign Relations*, 88th Cong., 1st Sess., March 25, 1963, p. 708; Vernon McKay, "South African Propaganda: Methods and Media," *Africa Report* 11, 2 (February 1966):41–46; William R. Cotter and Thomas Karis, "We Have Nothing to Hide," *Africa Report* 21, 6 (November–December 1976):37–45.

18. Noer, *Cold War and Black Liberation*, p. 140.

19. Schraeder, *United States Foreign Policy*, pp. 201–202.

20. Joseph Albright and Marcia Kunstel, "CIA Tip Led to '62 Arrest of Mandela: Ex-Official Tells of US Coup to Aid S. Africa," *Atlanta Constitution*, June 10, 1990.

21. Noer, *Cold War and Black Liberation*, p. 161.

22. "U.S. Judge Observes Trial in South Africa," *New York Times*, April 29, 1964; "UN Security Council Condemns Apartheid in South Africa," *State Department Bulletin* 51, 1306 (July 6, 1964):29–33.

23. Terrence Lyons, "Keeping Africa Off the Agenda," in Warren I. Cohen and Nancy Bernkopf Tucker, eds., *Lyndon Johnson Confronts the World: American Foreign Policy, 1963–1968* (New York: Cambridge University Press, 1994), pp. 245–278.

24. R.B.J. Walker, *One World, Many Worlds: Struggles for a Just World Peace* (Boulder: Lynne Rienner, 1988), pp. 81–114; Christian Joppke, *Mobilizing Against Nuclear Energy: A Comparison of Germany and the United States* (Berkeley and Los Angeles: University of California Press, 1993), pp. 16–17.

25. Mary-Louise Hopper, "The Johannesburg Bus Boycott," *Africa Today* 4 (November–December 1957):13–16.

26. "The Emergency Campaign," *Africa Today* 7 (May 1960):3.

27. George Houser, *No One Can Stop the Rain: Glimpses of Africa's Liberation Struggle* (New York: Pilgrim Press, 1989), p. 266.

28. "Correspondence," *Africa Today*, 12, 2 (February 1965):16; "American Campaign Against Apartheid Gets Underway: Students Demonstrate at Chase-Manhattan," *Africa Today* 12, 3 (March 1965):11; *New York Times*, July 23, 1965.

29. Kenneth Carstens, "The Response of the Church in the USA to Apartheid," *Africa Today* 13 (December 1966):19–22; James P. Findlay Jr., *Church People in the Struggle: The National Council of Churches* (New York: Oxford University Press, 1993).

30. Howard Tolley, "Interest Group Litigation to Enforce Human Rights," *Political Science Quarterly* 105, 4 (Winter 1990–1991):620.

31. George Houser, interview by Connie Field, Clarity Film Productions, Berkeley, p. 4.

32. Ibid.

33. Houser, *No One Can Stop the Rain*, p. 128.

34. Ibid., p. 267.

35. Ogene, *Interest Groups*, p. 117.

36. Memo from George Houser to the Executive Board of the American Committee on Africa, September 26, 1961, box 2, folder 13, American Committee on Africa Papers, Amistad Research Center, Tulane University, New Orleans, La. (hereafter cited as ACOA Papers).

37. Memo from George Houser to the Executive Board of the American Committee on Africa, October 10, 1961, box 1, folder 6, ACOA Papers.

38. Memo from Arthur Waskow to Executive Board of the American Committee on Africa, January 15, 1968, box 2, folder 23, ACOA Papers.

39. Minutes, Executive Board of the American Committee on Africa, October 14, 1968, box 2, folder 23, ACOA Papers.

40. Richard Espy, *The Politics of the Olympic Games* (Berkeley and Los Angeles: University of California Press, 1979), pp. 84–106.

41. Fred Block, *Postindustrial Possibilities: A Critique of Economic Discourse* (Berkeley and Los Angeles: University of California Press, 1990).

42. Walker, *One World, Many Worlds*, pp. 115–118; Michael Schudson, "Culture and the Integration of National Societies," *International Social Science Journal* 46 (February 1994):63–81.

43. Henry F. Jackson, *From the Congo to Soweto: U.S. Foreign Policy Toward Africa Since 1960* (New York: William Morrow, 1982); Martin Staniland, "Africa, the American Intelligentsia, and the Shadow of Vietnam," *Political Science Quarterly*

98, 4 (Winter 1983–1984):600; Deborah Stone, *Policy Paradox and Political Reason* (Glenview, Ill: Scott Foresman, 1988), pp. 108–116.

44. Noer, *Cold War and Black Liberation,* p. 181; Carstens, "The Response of the Church," pp. 6–7.

45. Roberta Garner and Mayer Zald, "The Political Economy and Social Movement Sectors," in Gerald D. Suttles and Mayer N. Zald, eds., *The Challenge of Social Control* (Norwood, N.J.: Ablex, 1985), p. 120.

46. *New York Times,* March 23, 1960.

47. Patrick Henry Martin, "American Views on South Africa, 1948–1972," Ph.D. diss., Louisiana State University, 1974, pp. 115–120.

48. David A. Snow and Robert D. Benford, "Ideology, Frame Resonance and Participant Mobilization," in *International Social Movement Research,* vol. 1 (Greenwich, Conn.: JAI Press, 1988), pp. 197–217; Hull, *American Enterprise in South Africa.*

49. Ogene, *Interest Groups,* pp. 153–158; Olav Stokke, *Reporting Africa* (New York: African Publishing, 1971), p. 12; Martin Staniland, "Who Needs African Studies?" *African Studies Review* 26, 3–4 (September–December 1983):77–97.

4

Benign Neglect to Global Threat: Creating Political Space for Anti-Apartheid Activism, 1969–1975

Well, that's the kind of popular conscious[ness]-raising that we did. The kind of creating avenues for people to speak and inform, creating avenues for people to write, to reflect, to get on radio shows, and, you know, a kind of important factor, I think, that strength and capacity to have the protest here in Washington, D.C.[1]

—Sylvia Hill, grassroots activist

Research on the Nixon administration's global realism emphasizes the way it relegated Africa to the periphery of foreign policy concerns and thus limited the visibility of domestic challenges to apartheid.[2] Yet closer examination reveals that international developments during the period dislodged Nixon's narrow construction of national priorities and opened up space for domestic critics to contest American ties to South Africa. As a result, an administration that had treated southern Africa with "benign neglect" in 1969 reinterpreted events in that region five years later as threats to U.S. global interests.

This chapter explores how the anti-apartheid movement capitalized on the blurring of distinctions between domestic and foreign politics and widened its access to a broad range of public and private policymaking arenas. This expansion exhibits three central elements outlined by political process theory. First, the political opportunity structure improved as South Africa grew more vulnerable to regional political pressures and experienced economic instability. Second, Presidents Nixon and Ford could not develop a national consensus on southern Africa, thus providing an opening for critics to create a new context for linking the region to post-Vietnam foreign policy generally. And third, new locally based groups and new southern Africa programs created by existing protest organizations swelled the organizational base of anti-apartheid activism.

The Political Opportunity Structure

South Africa was not a major campaign issue in 1968, but the outcomes of the presidential and congressional elections had important implications for the anti-apartheid movement. The first hurdle arose with the election of Richard Nixon, who had campaigned on the theme that the United States needed restoration of "law and order," both at home and abroad. The administration extended the powers of domestic law enforcement agencies to control dissent, simultaneously attacking revolutionary insurgency in Southeast Asia and bringing Laos and Cambodia into the Vietnam War. The African component of this new version of containment policy emerged from National Security Study Memorandum No. 39 (NSSM).

NSSM-39, secretly labeled the "Tar Baby" option, consisted of a comprehensive review of Southern Africa policies prepared by the staff of national security adviser Henry Kissinger. It outlined five options:

1. developing stronger relationships with the white regimes, while ignoring their domestic policies as factors in deciding U.S. relations,
2. encouraging communication with the white regimes, rather than ostracism, as a way of producing moderate change in their domestic policies,
3. symbolic disassociation from the white regimes, but maintaining substantial relationships with them,
4. a substantial reduction in ties with the white states,
5. adoption of a lower profile and reduction of the U.S. presence in the region.[3]

The administration chose option two, which advocated closer ties to the white settler governments in South Africa and Rhodesia and with the Portuguese colonies of Angola and Mozambique. The policy derived from two assumptions: (1) Africans did not pose a credible threat to the colonial regimes, and (2) the Soviet Union would not intervene in the region. The new guidelines enabled sales of aircraft and other technical equipment to South Africa formerly prohibited under the terms of an earlier UN arms embargo. These changes also encouraged U.S. businesses to increase transactions with South Africa. After a decade of American rhetorical support for continued decolonization, the Nixon tilt toward the white states presented an additional obstacle for anti-apartheid activism.

Throughout the 1960s, the high profit rates of American companies in South Africa encouraged significant reinvestment. Those profits enabled businesses to buy controlling interests in South African firms and operate wholly owned subsidiaries. As the industrial economy matured, American entrepreneurs responded enthusiastically by shifting significant portions of their investments to the growing manufacturing sector (Table 4.1).

By the mid-1960s the South African economy had recuperated from the instability and uncertainty that followed the Sharpeville massacre, achieving one of the highest growth rates in the world. This remarkable turnaround resulted from two interrelated developments, one economic and one political. Economically, South Africa continued to attract substantial foreign capital and technology, allowing it to enlarge the industrial infrastructure.[4] Through an expanded and articulated state sector, the government played an active role in redistributing the costs and benefits of prosperity. Afrikaner social mobility, for example, depended largely on employment opportunities created by an enlarged state bureaucracy, especially in the security complex designed to control the black population.[5] Politically, state security forces stabilized one of the economy's vital inputs—superexploitable black labor—and effectively crushed black political resistance for nearly fifteen years.

Profit rates in the manufacturing sector remained high for American companies, and they also illustrate U.S. capital's deepening connection to one of apartheid's inherent contradictions. The rapid growth in manufacturing weakened the overall apartheid goal of separate development. The "pull" of jobs in the urban manufacturing economy, combined with the "push" of poverty from the rural homelands, intensified black migration into white-designated areas. South Africa had not come closer to

TABLE 4.1   U.S. Direct Investment in the Republic of South Africa, 1968–1975

Year	Book Value (million $)
1968	692.00
1969	775.00
1970	778.00
1971	875.00
1972	941.00
1973	1.24
1974	1.47
1975	1.58

SOURCE: U.S. Department of Commerce, *Statistical Abstract of the United States* (Washington, D.C.: 1968–1976).

achieving racial separatism by 1970 because the black population in urban areas had tripled and exceeded that of whites.[6]

The South African economy's dependence on a black urban labor force created two additional problems. The sizable "illegal" population required further expansion of the enormous bureaucracy of police, courts, and labor administrators. This army of public-sector employees further drained the public treasury, putting pressure on the state to make the enterprise more cost-effective. In addition, in contrast to agriculture and mining, manufacturing required a flexible workforce more adaptable to industrial regimentation and training.

The responsibility for producing this workforce fell upon the state bureaucracy and its educational system. Both the education system and the manufacturing sector further demonstrated the inequalities of apartheid. African secondary education grew in 1970 in response to skilled labor shortages. Some black students were even allowed to enroll in white universities. Developing the system required additional public expenditure, which never kept pace with the rapid increase in enrollments. Chronic shortages of classrooms and qualified teachers consequently led to lowered quality in education, thereby raising production costs to the manufacturing sector.[7]

Efforts to train urban black residents to fill the lower tiers of the labor force altered their structural location in the economy and indirectly introduced new political socialization processes. The African population remained fairly quiescent throughout the 1960s, but a political reawakening began in the early 1970s as the Black Consciousness movement (BCM)[8] energized college and high-school students. BCM consisted of an amalgam of ideas and elements absorbed from indigenous movements and from black American activism. The state initially tolerated BCM, believing that it represented a form of separatism compatible with basic apartheid principles. Gradually, BCM assumed a more revolutionary posture, becoming a mass movement that penetrated the lower levels of the segregated school system and providing the ideological foundations for a radical challenge to apartheid.

Another form of black resistance—the trade union movement—also resurfaced in the 1970s as inequalities in wages and working conditions between blacks and whites worsened.[9] Black workers also mobilized against the extensive system of pass controls that curtailed family contacts for much of the year and undermined the social and economic fabric of black communities. The first strike wave began in 1973 in Durban, one of the country's major industrial regions. The Durban strikes are significant because they remained spontaneous: Workers avoided co-optation by refusing to elect leaders. The strikers avoided taking any explicit political position and protected their organizational structure from scrutiny by mobilizing factory by factory, from the bottom up. Durban thus represented a new stage in trade unionism, and there, the movement exploited black labor's strategic location during a key stage in the maturation of South Africa's economy. It succeeded by dodging the wrath of the state's repressive apparatus.

The maturing South African industrial economy indirectly enhanced the mobilization potential of black students and workers. The growth of its tourist sector similarly made the role of foreign capital and markets visible and furnished targets for apartheid's adversaries. The American Express Company initiated tours to South Africa in the late 1920s, but the high cost of travel ended the experiment after just a few years. Substantial reductions in travel time between the United States and South Africa by the late 1940s rejuvenated tourism. South African Airways established regular flights from Johannesburg to New York in the mid-1950s, and Pan Am Airways initiated service a few years later. Western International Hotels, a division of United Airlines, and Holiday Inn entered South Africa in the late 1960s. The country's well-organized game parks and resorts attracted American tourists. Passenger volume increased steadily and then accelerated in 1973, when the acquisition of Boeing 747s by both South African Airways and Pan American shortened flying time to less than fourteen hours. Anti-apartheid activists focused on the disparity between the well-organized tourist version of South Africa and the brutal system required to maintain it.[10]

Nixon administration policies and corporate investment patterns suggested a commitment to work with the apartheid system, but domestic developments in the late 1960s created more opportunities for addressing racial inequality in southern Africa. The 1968 congressional elections abetted anti-apartheid activism in two key areas. First, the seniority system made Michigan Democrat Charles C. Diggs chair of the House Subcommittee on Africa in the 91st Congress. Diggs, the first African American to head the subcommittee, turned it into a forum where anti-apartheid issues could develop policy momentum. He conducted hearings on topics such as UN sanctions against Rhodesia, U.S. business involvement in South Africa, and political repression in both states. As chair, Diggs led fact-finding missions to southern Africa and regularly invited anti-apartheid groups, civil rights and human rights organizations, Africanist scholars, and African liberation support groups to contribute to subcommittee meetings.

Second, the formation of the Congressional Black Caucus (CBC) in 1971 enhanced black power in Congress.[11] The number of black representatives increased from four in 1960 to thirteen in 1971. Although domestic policy concerns dominated CBC's agenda, its participation in the expanding constituency for African issues further defined and validated the foreign policy interests of African Americans. The establishment of CBC coincided with a series of congressional reforms that expanded the committee system, increased professional staff size and resources, and improved support services such as the Congressional Research Service. The legislative body was thus able to match more effectively the powers of the executive branch.

Nixon's containment policies relegated Africa to the margins of foreign policy but as two clashes between the administration and Congress demonstrate, domestic politics could not be entirely shielded from African questions. The 1971 controversy over efforts to renew South Africa's sugar quota and the Ford administration's covert involvement in the Angolan civil war in 1975 provided opportunities to draw public attention to apartheid and colonialism. When these issues came to a head, momentum rapidly shifted from the executive to the legislative branch as the Subcommittee on Africa brought oppositional discourses into the policy debate.

Since 1962, the Department of Agriculture had allowed South Africa's sugar industry to participate in a program that guaranteed it a percentage of the stateside market. In that year, South African sugar represented just over 1 percent of all sugar imports (Table 4.2).[12] This increased to nearly 20 percent in 1963 and 1965. By 1970, South African sugar, worth nearly $5 million, totaled over 6 percent of the foreign sugar on the domestic market. A 1965 amendment to the Sugar Act that extended the South African quota came under fire from anti-apartheid activists and liberal members of the House and Senate in the late 1960s.

TABLE 4.2   South African Sugar Exports to the United States

Year	Tons
1962	97,727
1963	132,272
1964	119,960
1965	103,862
1966	72,892
1967	70,863
1968	67,512
1969	59,595
1970	76,649
1971	69,860
1972	59,656
1973	74,535
1974	60,440

SOURCE: U.S. Department of Agriculture, Agricultural Stabilization and Conservation Service, *Sugar Statistics and Related Data* (Washington, D.C.: 1970–1975).

Opposition to a South African quota had originated with a 1961 protest lodged by the American Negro Leadership Conference on Africa with G. Mennen Williams, assistant secretary of state for African affairs. Letters sent to Secretary of Agriculture Orville Freeman, Secretary of State Dean Rusk, and UN ambassador Adlai Stevenson merited perfunctory replies that South African sugar purchases did not contradict official opposition to apartheid. The ACOA, the Congressional Black Caucus, the NAACP, church-based groups, and liberal legislators, including Massachusetts senator Edward Kennedy and New York Democratic congressmen John Dow and Jonathan Bingham, swung into action. They mounted a campaign using speeches, articles, and expert witness before congressional committees to eliminate the quota. Americans who purchased South African sugar, they argued, underwrote the severe exploitation of black field-workers and subsidized apartheid.[13]

Sugar quota opponents faced several obstacles in their effort to ensure that pro–South Africa amendments to the Sugar Act expired on schedule at the end of 1971. Nixon's rapprochement with South Africa, as outlined by NSSM-39, had already begun. The Department of Agriculture, with its predominantly rural and agribusiness constituencies,[14] saw South Africa as one more external opportunity for U.S. businesses. The congressional committee chairs responsible for sugar quota legislation, W. R. Poage (D.–Tex.) of the House Agriculture Committee and Russell Long (D.–La.) of the Senate Finance Committee, represented the rural, racist interests that had impeded civil rights legislation a decade earlier.

Finally, lobbyists for South Africa, presented a less visible yet still formidable barrier to opponents of the sugar allocation. The South African Sugar Association (SASA) relied on the South African embassy, the South African Foundation, and representatives of companies conducting business in that country for support. SASA also retained the New York law firm Casey, Lane and Mittendorf to represent its stateside interests. John R. Mahoney, who handled the SASA account, prepared reports and position papers for key decisionmakers in the State Department, the Department of Agriculture, and Congress, especially members of the House Agriculture Committee. The firm made political donations to presidential and congressional candidates of both parties and spent over $160,000 in the 1971 drive to renew Pretoria's sugar allocation.[15]

The sugar quota controversy furnished one of the first clear opportunities for anti-apartheid activists to penetrate the policymaking process. Yet the diverse coalition of groups could not overcome the advantages of organization, resources, and access to policymakers that South African interests enjoyed. In emphasizing South Africa's loyalty to the West, its fervent anticommunism, and its economic productivity, the lobbyists derailed oppositional efforts to inject human rights into policy considerations.[16]

If the sugar allocation battle was a defeat for activists, the sudden collapse of Portugal's African empire in 1974 pushed southern Africa from the margin to the center of policy debates. Portuguese-controlled Angola and Mozambique were strategic holdings in the area often viewed as a white cordon sanitaire against the spread of African independence movements.[17] Whereas other European colonial powers made plans for the postwar dissolution of their empires in Africa, the Portuguese dictatorship demonstrated no such inclination well into the 1970s.

A succession of presidents from Roosevelt to Nixon adopted a middle-road strategy between support for Portugal and assistance to independence movements in its territories. As liberation movements escalated attacks against the colonial governments in Angola and Mozambique, Portugal began to unravel militarily, politically, and economically. Its weakness was felt both at home and in the colonies. The dissolution of the regime ironically coincided with the decline of U.S. involvement in Southeast Asia and provided a symbolic link between the two regions.[18]

A comprehensive analysis of the Angolan civil war is beyond the scope of this study, but touching on aspects of it offer insights into gains in momentum made by anti-apartheid activism when deeper internationalization of the war drew the United States into a series of dubious relationships. The April 1974 overthrow of the Caetano dictatorship in Portugal led an interim government to grant independence to its African colonies. The government of Portugal and liberation representatives in Mozambique and Guinea-Bissau developed plans for an orderly transition of power, but the settlement in Angola disintegrated in March 1975, when the internecine struggle among the three liberation groups Movimento Popular de Libertação de Angola (MPLA), Frente Nacional de Libertação de Angola (FNLA), and União Nacional para a Independência Total de Angola (UNITA) revived.

The choices selected from the NSSM-39 inventory blinded American policymakers to scenarios other than a continued Portuguese presence in southern Africa and left them unprepared to respond to a war impervious to great power control. The Cold War impulses of the CIA and other agencies dictated opposing MPLA, the Marxist faction, which the Soviet Union and Cuba, among other states, supported. In July 1974, nearly six months before fighting erupted, the CIA began supplying covert aid to FNLA, which also received assistance from the People's Republic of China and Zaire, itself a U.S. client state. According to former CIA agent John Stockwell, head of the Angola Task Force, these approaches to FNLA remained largely symbolic. They were meant to exhibit Washington's capacity to deal itself into the battle for Angola and belie any appearance of a post-Vietnam malaise.[19] The United States eventually sent more than $30 million in weapons and aid to Angolan rebel factions.

Anxieties over the war in Angola led the United States to reinforce its ties to two of its most trusty allies in the region, Zaire and South Africa. Zairian president Mobutu Sese Seko, a U.S. client since the early 1960s, did not see the war as an opportunity to remove one of the last wedges of colonialism from Africa but as a chance to enhance his sizable personal fortune. In the name of regional security, Mobutu successfully convinced an apprehensive Ford administration and Secretary of State Henry Kissinger to increase military aid to Zaire from $3.4 million in 1975 to $30 million in 1977. He also acquired a Security Support Assistance package worth more than $60 million.[20]

The administration also relied on South Africa as a stabilizing force in Angola. Pretoria, which backed UNITA (as did China, and later the United States), stepped up its involvement in the war by sending a 5,000-man force, composed of mercenaries, troops from UNITA and FNLA, and its regular army, to Angola in October 1975. Cuba, determined to assist its socialist ally MPLA, began airlifting supplies and thousands of soldiers to Angola. In less than two years, covert actions underwritten by the Ford administration to bolster containment strategies evolved into a close cooperative relationship with South Africa just when regional racial conflict began attracting more international attention.

President Ford tried to conceal U.S. involvement in Angola from the public even while the international spotlight focused on that troubled country. Tensions among various factions in the administration meanwhile threatened to expose the entanglements. In late 1974, Ford fired Donald Easum, assistant secretary of state for African affairs, partially for his public acknowledgment that the United States could live with an MPLA government. Ford then nominated Nathaniel Davis, former U.S. ambassador to Chile, as a replacement. This routine appointment came under unexpected public scrutiny because of Davis's presence in Santiago when the Allende government was overthrown. The naming of Davis caused speculation about his transfer to such a sensitive post. Criticisms did not abate when Davis resigned less than six months later, after taking a position on the Angolan war resembling Easum's.[21]

Growing involvement in southern Africa accompanied a post-Watergate period of skepticism about executive branch motives. A newly assertive Congress proved ready to launch inquiries into executive branch abuses. When rising public dissatisfaction forced the administration to break its silence on Angola, Kissinger disclosed the covert operations in Angola to the Senate and requested additional aid to the mission. Congress denied the request. In December 1975, the Senate attached the Clark Amendment (named after the chair of the subcommittee on Africa) to the 1976 Foreign Assistance Act. This amendment cut off all aid to guerrilla factions in Angola, imposing constraints on administration options and calling into question the president's ability to define U.S. interest in southern Africa.[22]

Organizational Developments

The controversies ignited by policy debacles in Angola and Vietnam coincided with public anxieties about institutional responses to Watergate. As both resonated with themes raised by anti-apartheid activists, mobilization costs dropped considerably as the movement penetrated new domains of American life.[23] The transformation of anti-apartheid activism from a fledging collection of groups dependent upon crises abroad into an assertive, multifaceted movement resulted from gains in four areas: shareholder resolutions, community-based activism, lobbying, and greater knowledge generation and dissemination capacity.

ACOA had been the principal national group organizing opposition to apartheid immediately after the Sharpeville crisis. A more diverse set of groups emerged in the mid-1960s to enlarge the sites and forms of action available for anti-apartheid protests. This development occurred during a period of veritable advocacy group explosion, with new group formations and mainstream social advocacy community reorganization in response to changes in the domestic and international political climate. A new generation of leadership emerged among religious, academic, legal, and public interest constituencies and extended its civil rights and social justice agenda to include racial inequality in southern Africa. This growth enabled the movement to develop a wider range of critical intervention skills and more elaborate mechanisms for holding the state and corporations accountable for their behavior at home and abroad.[24]

Shareholder activism as a weapon in the struggle against apartheid began in 1966 when the National Council of Churches encouraged members to review their investments in corporations involved in South Africa. But the potency of the strategy increased in 1970 when the Securities and Exchange Commission ruled that shareholders could submit resolutions on specific social responsibility concerns.[25] Investors relied upon two major types of resolution for introducing these concerns at stockholders' meetings: fact-finding, which requested that the corporation disclose its operations in South Africa or that it create investigative committees to examine the impact of corporate activities on black South Africans; and calls for unconditional termination of all activities in South Africa.

One of the first church-sponsored shareholder resolutions in 1971 asked GM to end its activities in South Africa. The resolution received only about 1 percent of the shares voted, but it generated considerable publicity that reverberated far beyond the meeting room. The National

Council of Churches, responding to increased member demand for information about corporate social responsibility, established the Corporate Information Center (CIC) in 1971. CIC merged with the Interfaith Committee on Corporate Responsibility in 1972 to form the Interfaith Center on Corporate Responsibility (ICCR). ICCR helped churches coordinate efforts to influence corporate conduct. Besides shareholder resolutions, ICCR strategies to restrict U.S. corporate activity in South Africa included letter-writing campaigns, meetings with management, offering testimony to congressional committees, requesting disclosures of information, and exploring alternative socially conscious investment possibilities. Over the next four years, shareholders directed resolutions at corporations such as GM, International Telephone and Telegraph (ITT), American Telephone and Telegraph (AT&T), American Metal Climax (AMAX), Union Carbide, Ford, Goodyear, Kraft, Polaroid, Sears, Xerox, Burroughs, International Business Machines (IBM), Mobil, and Exxon.[26]

Shareholder resolutions added a significant dimension to anti-apartheid activism. They demonstrated the movement's ability to sustain a national campaign that focused public attention on the linkages among transnational corporate behavior, domestic institutional investment, and apartheid. Furthermore, this form of activism lowered the costs of participation by giving broad segments of the middle class the means to subject businesses to public scrutiny. As shareholders pursued more proactive courses of action, it forced firms to explain and defend their role in the South African economy and society.

A similar strategy designed to force companies to disclose their South African operations emerged when black employees at the Polaroid Corporation headquarters in Cambridge, Massachusetts, formed the Polaroid Revolutionary Workers' Movement (PRWM) in 1970. PRWM, responding to the company's production and processing of film used in the South African government's passbook system, attempted to organize a boycott of Polaroid products and expose the company's segregated labor practices in South Africa. PRWM successfully pressured Polaroid to improve working conditions at its South African plants and offer 500 scholarships to black South African students.[27]

The ACOA supported a black popular component in the anti-apartheid movement by funding two additional field programs, one in Newark, New Jersey, headed by Ken Butler, and another in Chicago, directed by Prexy Nesbitt. Butler and Nesbitt cultivated southern African interests in the black community, as Blyden Jackson did in the New York–area program. They also worked on multiracial coalitions joining liberals and labor in their respective field sites.

Chicago, a traditional stronghold of black activism, proved especially receptive to mobilization on southern Africa. Nesbitt collaborated with area organizations such as the SCLC's Operation Breadbasket and with high-school teachers, colleges, churches, and civic groups, offering workshops and seminars. Two local groups, the African American Solidarity Committee, and the Chicago Committee for the Liberation of Angola, Mozambique, and Guinea-Bissau, a predominantly white organization, and an information source, the New World Resources Center, resulted from that experience.[28]

Despite the success of these field programs, tensions marked ACOA's relationship with the black community. A special executive board meeting called in October 1970 addressed some of these difficulties. Blyden Jackson, the field staffer in the New York program, felt that "the heart of the problem is that ACOA has a radical and black staff working for a white, liberal organization. But the staff has little role in the formation of policy and is cut off from this function."[29]

Eileen Hanson, who replaced Nesbitt after his departure from ACOA in 1971, echoed Jackson's concerns. Hanson contended that field-workers felt detached from the central office and isolated from current developments in southern Africa, as well as within the growing African-American Africanist constituency that could strengthen their efforts in the black community. Additionally, she argued that as ACOA had no local history, many in the black community viewed it with suspicion.[30]

African-American staffers in other predominantly white organizations expressed similar anxieties. Jerry Herman, one of the first blacks to work with the American Friends Service Committee's (AFSC) southern African program, felt that its activist orientation varied from his own civil rights–based mobilization strategy: "I think they saw it a little bit differently—I think they saw it as working with other organizations, interacting, building bridges. And my history had not really been about that; it had always been about organizing at the grassroots level and hooking all of that together."[31]

These groups had worthy objectives, according to Herman, but they exhibited a politically naïveté that impaired movement development: "What I found out was that [with] a lot of the national organizations working on these issues, there was not very much depth—they really did not understand Africa or African issues. It was kind of the right thing to do and I think there was a bit of romanticism of the struggles that were taking place rather than real people on the ground struggling about real issues just like in their community."[32]

Southern Africa appeared prominently on the agenda of numerous black organizations in the early 1970s, including the Congress of African People, the Africa Information Service, the African-American Scholars Council, the African Heritage Studies Association, and the Pan-African Liberation Committee.[33] The National Black Political Convention, held in

Gary, Indiana, in March 1972, devoted considerable attention to U.S. policy toward South Africa. The convention produced an uneasy coalition between black elected officials, particularly the Congressional Black Caucus, and black nationalist and community-based activists. The African Liberation Support Committee (ALSC), which organized African Liberation Day marches in Washington, D.C., and thirty other cities around the nation in 1972 and 1973, resulted from that collaboration.

The ALSC initially put its energies into providing support for the Angolan and Mozambican liberation movements in their struggle against Portugal but eventually became a critical site for sensitizing black American communities to racial inequality in southern Africa. Sylvia Hill, a Washington, D.C.–based activist recalled that

> there were some kind of building blocks already established. You know, for example, when we came back, we started, I think it was called National Southern Africa Coordinating Committee. We didn't have a local base but we were thinking big, right. So we finally realized that, well, it's really hard to have a national group if you don't have a local base. So let's just decide we're going to organize locally, first. And we were a group of women, in large part. Initially we had what was called the Southern Africa News Collective and we met twice a week. And just studied how to organize, looked at different models of organizing around the world and began to write a newsletter about how to organize. And then decided, well, we need to be really organizing ourselves. So we created this group called the Southern Africa Summer Project, mind you. And we were gonna use refugee issues to kind of mobilize some popular consciousness about what was happening in Southern Africa, really.[34]

According to Hill, reaching out to liberation movements in southern Africa and simultaneously refining domestic mobilization strategies proved quite useful:

> And learning from . . . studying the liberation movements of MPLA and FRELIMO [Front for the Liberation of Mozambique] and PAIGC [African Party for the Independence of Guinea and Cape Verde] and so forth [was] very instructive about [how] we should model our organizations and how we should really begin to think more carefully about organizing and planning. That it was something scientific and you didn't just, you know, kind of willy-nilly along, hoping that people would fall in and do the right thing and such. So we did study those groups a great deal, and we did the Mozambique Film Project where we tried to show films. One of the decisive features, I think, of international . . . decisive moments in our capacity to do conscious[ness]-raising in this country around the liberation movements

was the making of *A Luta Continua* by Van Lierop. Because that film enabled us to kind of carry, you know, something visual around as such. Later, we did, not films, but, you know, slide shows and those kinds of visuals and all that to convey what was happening in Zimbabwe, Rhodesia, at that time, Namibia.[35]

During the same period, black members of the International Long-shoremen and Warehouse Union and the Coalition of Black Trade Unionists mobilized opposition to collaboration with the colonial states in southern Africa. Longshoremen and Southern University students in 1972 demonstrated in Burnside, Louisiana, a port north of New Orleans, against the unloading of ships carrying Rhodesian chrome. Similar actions unfolded in Boston, New York, Philadelphia, and Baltimore, from fall 1973 to spring 1974.[36] Many of these efforts did not result in permanent organizations, but the temporary expressive outlets they provided tapped into latent elements of the Africanist constituency and expanded the potential for mobilization in black communities.

Nixon administration rapprochement toward the white regimes in southern Africa served as a reminder of the dearth of meaningful structural access by anti-apartheid groups. ACOA took a major step in addressing that problem in 1972 by establishing the Washington Office on Africa (WOA) as a permanent lobby. ACOA created WOA, but its sponsors included various churches—Methodist, Episcopalian, Presbyterian, and United Church of Christ—and labor unions.[37] Edgar Lockwood, an

Norfolk, Virginia, churchwomen preparing to ship clothing to refugees of the Zimbabwe-Rhodesian civil war in 1974. Diverse constituencies mobilized around racial inequality in southern Africa during expansion of the movement's action repertoire.

SOURCE: *Southern Africa,* 1974.

Episcopalian minister and a lawyer, became its first executive director. WOA provided congressional testimony, supplied issue briefs on Southern Africa to members and staffers, and produced a monthly newsletter, *Washington Notes on Africa,* to keep the anti-apartheid constituency abreast of policy developments. The construction of a lobbying apparatus, combined with the Congressional Black Caucus and Diggs's assumption of the chair of the House Subcommittee on Africa, offered anti-apartheid activists limited but regular access to the congressional forum.[38]

By late 1975, a network of groups had developed that could respond to growing political conflict in southern Africa. The decentralized pattern of the movement's organizational development had not been without its problems, though, especially during the early 1970s. For example, anti-apartheid activists viewed the 1971 hearings on the renewal of South Africa's sugar quota allocation as a major test of congressional opinion on U.S. ties to South Africa. Many movement groups participated in the revocation effort. ACOA, besides providing testimony before the congressional committee, prepared issue briefs, conducted research, and contacted the legislative assistants of more than 100 members of the House. The Task Force on South Africa, a coalition composed of the

United Mine Workers at the 1974 Southern Company stockholders' meeting in Birmingham, Alabama, protesting the company's decision to buy South African coal. This protest reflected organized labor's efforts to link domestic worker struggles to exploitation abroad.

SOURCE: *Southern Africa,* 1974.

AFSC, the United Presbyterian Church, and the ADA, mobilized extensively around the hearings.

The minimal contribution of other components of the network, however, and the overall lack of coordination, undermined the movement's ability to match the strong pro–South African lobby.[39] A similar situation occurred with the campaign to overturn the Byrd Amendment, which allowed the importation of Rhodesian chrome in defiance of a UN ban. In both cases, activists made an impressive showing but could not match the money, influence, and power of South African and Rhodesian–backed lobbyists. The decisionmaking locus in both issues shifted away from the State Department to congressional committees such as those for agriculture and armed services, traditionally dominated by anti–civil rights, Southern, conservative, and Republican legislators with little sympathy for an Africanist constituency.

In spite of their inability to dislodge policymakers from Cold War constructions of Africa, the anti-apartheid constituency refined its ability to appeal to an American public amenable to alternative ways of viewing U.S. connections to southern Africa. The confidence with which activists approached the region reflected the existence of a knowledge base that had not existed a decade earlier. Anti-apartheid and anticolonial groups relied implicitly on a growing and vital field of African studies well equipped to benefit from the public salience of the southern Africa controversies.

The major growth spurt of African studies occurred before the 1970s wave of armed African independence movements (Figure 4.1). This growth coincided with the establishment of area studies and black studies programs. These subfields introduced new problems, research questions, discourses, scholars, journals, and controversies that laid the foundations for launching critical intervention strategies into the traditional academic and policymaker constructions of Africa. Many professionally trained Africanists prided themselves on the seamless flow of their scholarly and political commitments and joined such groups as the African Heritage Studies Association and the Association of Concerned Africanist Scholars (ACAS).[40]

The incorporation of knowledge about Africa into the mainstream academy meant that activists could take greater risks in charting a course of action. Not all activists perceived academic "respectability," however, as necessarily important. Many felt that real change in U.S. behavior in the region would result only from pressure from ordinary citizens. Additionally, activism seldom, if ever, emerges from a single blueprint. Advocates experiment with different approaches, often tailored to the community, the issue, or the opportunity of the moment.[41] Sponsoring organizations and leaders may invest time and resources in a particular

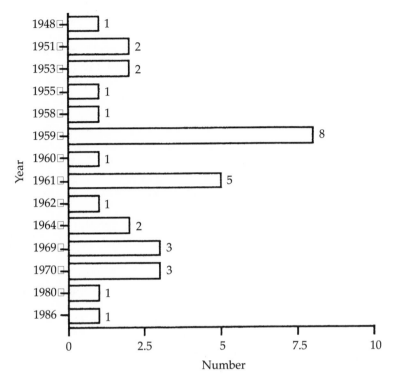

FIGURE 4.1   Growth of African Studies Programs, 1948–1986

SOURCE: *Directory of African and Afro-American Studies Programs, 1986, Seventh Edition* (Waltham, Mass.: African Studies Association, 1987).

issue, community, or moment but may never see a direct return in increased membership or new contributions toward that investment. These investments nevertheless often go a long way toward raising consciousness and taking individuals beyond anywhere a sponsoring organization is prepared to go. ACOA, as one board member argued, continually faced the challenge of expanding its capacity to wait for this "invisible return."[42]

Consciousness-Raising

Historically, concern about the problems generated by apartheid failed to penetrate domestic politics beyond a brief crisis stage.[43] Consequently, anti-apartheid activists experienced initial feelings of powerlessness that gradually gave way to willingness to work collectively and use the policymaking process to implement change. They necessarily depended on openings provided by established institutions, as well as relying on movement initiatives. Between Nixon's inauguration in 1969 and the first year of Gerald Ford's presidency, American domestic institutions experienced significant changes that enhanced the structural access of anti-apartheid activists. The Congressional Black Caucus, the House subcommittee on Africa, and the House Subcommittee on International Organizations and Movements, developed as major points of access for the anti-apartheid community. The collapse of the Portuguese empire and the termination of American involvement in Southeast Asia undermined endorsements for the status quo in U.S. foreign policy. Congressional resistance to Ford administration pressures to intervene in Angola provided further evidence that government can be an agent of change. A November 1975 Harris poll indicated growing convergence of opinion between a substantial sector of the public and the anti-apartheid community on intervention in Angola.[44]

Grassroots networks expanded dramatically in the early 1970s to strengthen the connections between local- and national-level protest initiatives to complement the gains made at the policymaking level. The cultural arm of the movement began to target South African attempts to gain legitimacy through tourism and films. In September 1974, the New York City Human Rights Commission ruled in favor of the ACOA's complaint that the *New York Times* had violated the city's human rights guidelines by running advertisements for South African tourism and employment.[45]

Anti-apartheid organizations could also boast of having secured firmer access to the congressional policymaking process. The congressional class of 1974, elected in the aftermath of Nixon's resignation and the Watergate scandals, provided further encouragement for anti-apartheid activists to become involved in electoral politics and lobbying. After Congress rejected Ford's appeal for funds to intervene in the Angolan civil war, the Washington Office on Africa opined that "the gratifying gains show that electing the right person and educating him or her on southern African issues may be more effective and easier than converting incumbents who have an established position."[46]

The pursuit of the movement's instrumental objectives often yielded secondary consciousness-raising effects. Sylvia Hill, for example, argues that activism constituted an effective means of deepening African-American group understanding of Pan-African connections:

> [W]e continued to have a kind of belief that this was an important solidarity moment in our history, and once we became more and more involved, we started doing quite a bit of historical research. And then began to see some of the, aside from Du Bois, that we knew of, Paul Robeson, you know, in that

sense, but then really began to see some of the kind of interactions that had taken place between NAACP and the ANC, for example. The visits that the Marcus Garvey movement had sponsored of Namibians and South Africans throughout the United States, and so we were kind of stunned that, well, this has been going on, we're just following in the tradition. And we didn't know about it—we had no sense of that history.[47]

Conclusion

The European and southern African power redistribution in the mid-1970s, attendant on the collapse of the Portuguese dictatorship, the withdrawal from Vietnam, and the internationalization of war in Angola and Mozambique, undermined the foundations of the post–World War II political and economic order. Anti-apartheid activists capitalized on this series of political jolts to become legitimate contenders in selected local and national policymaking arenas. Mobilizing an array of instruments—shareholder resolutions, lobbying, and dissemination of critical information—activists penetrated previously restricted spaces. Access did not consistently translate into influence because disparities in resources and skill enabled South Africa and its support apparatus to shield apartheid from complete scrutiny.

Notes

1. Sylvia Hill, interview by Connie Field, Clarity Film Productions, Berkeley, 1996, p. 12.

2. Christopher Coker, *The United States and South Africa, 1968–1985: Constructive Engagement and Its Critics* (Durham, N.C.: Duke University Press, 1986).

3. Anthony Lake, *The "Tar Baby" Option: American Policy Toward Southern Rhodesia* (New York: Columbia University Press, 1976), p. 124.

4. Sergio Vieira, William G. Martin, and Immanuel Wallerstein, eds., *How Fast the Wind: Southern Africa, 1975–2000* (Trenton, N.J.: Africa World Press, 1992), pp. 165–196.

5. Hermann Giliomee, "The Afrikaner Advance," in Heribert Adam and Herman Giliomee, *Ethnic Power Mobilized* (New Haven: Yale University Press, 1979), p. 171.

6. Robert Price, *The Apartheid State in Crisis, 1975–1990* (New York: Oxford University Press, 1991), pp. 29–31.

7. John Marcum, *Education, Race, and Change in South Africa* (Berkeley and Los Angeles: University of California Press, 1982), p. 4.

8. Robert Fatton Jr., *Black Consciousness in South Africa* (Albany: SUNY Press, 1986), pp. 67–68.

9. Tom Lodge, *Black Politics in South Africa Since 1945* (New York: Longman, 1983), pp. 326–327.

10. Richard Hull, *American Enterprise in South Africa* (New York: New York University Press, 1990), pp. 222–224, 284; William R. Cotter and Thomas Karis, "We Have Nothing to Hide," *Africa Report* 21, 6 (November–December 1976):37–45.

11. Jake Miller, "Black Legislators and African-American Relations," *Journal of Black Studies* 20 (1979):245–261.

12. U.S. Department of Agriculture, Agricultural Stabilization and Conservation Service, *Sugar Statistics and Related Data*, February 1970.

13. American Committee on Africa, "The U.S. Should End the South African Sugar Quota and Stop Buying Sugar from South Africa," 1971, American Committee on Africa Papers, Amistad Research Center, Tulane University, New Orleans, La. (hereafter cited as ACOA Papers).

14. James A. Thurber, "Dynamics of Policy Subsystems in American Politics," in Allan J. Cigler and Burdett A. Loomis, *Interest Group Politics,* 3d ed. (Washington, D.C.: Congressional Quarterly Press, 1991), pp. 330–333.

15. F. Chodozie Ogene, *Interest Groups and the Shaping of Foreign Policy: Four Case Studies of United States Foreign Policy* (New York: St. Martin's Press, 1983), p. 171; John Felton, "South Africa Sugar Lobby Admits Gifts to Members of House Agricultural Panel," *Congressional Quarterly Weekly Report* 36, 35 (September 2, 1978):2367.

16. In June 1974, Congress voted to terminate the Sugar Act as a result of consumer group charges that it artificially inflated prices. "Sugar Legislation Dies," *Congressional Weekly Quarterly Report* 36, 42 (October 21, 1974):1; "Sugar Bill Death Sweetens South Africa's Profits," *Southern Africa* 7, 7 (July–August 1974):29.

17. Immanuel Wallerstein and Sergio Vieira, "Historical Development of the Region in the Context of the Evolving World System," in Vieira, Martin, and Wallerstein, *How Fast the Wind*, p. 12.

18. John Marcum, *The Angolan Revolution: Exile Politics and Guerrilla Warfare, 1962–1976*, vol. 2 (Boston: MIT Press, 1978); Martin Staniland, "Africa, the American Intelligentsia, and the Shadow of Vietnam," *Political Science Quarterly* 98 (Winter 1983–1984):595–616.

19. John Stockwell, *In Search of Enemies: A CIA Story* (New York: W. W. Norton, 1978), p. 67.

20. Peter J. Schraeder, *United States Foreign Policy Toward Africa: Incrementalism, Crisis, and Change* (New York: Cambridge University Press, 1994), pp. 84–86.

21. Nathaniel Davis, "The Angolan Decision of 1975: A Personal Memoir," *Foreign Affairs* 57, 1 (Fall 1978):109–124.

22. U.S. Congress, Senate, *Select Committee to Study Governmental Operations with Respect to Intelligence Activities*, 94th Cong., 2d sess., 1976; United States Senate, Committee on Foreign Relations, *U.S. Involvement in the Civil War in Angola. Hearings*, 94th Cong., 2d sess., January 29, February 3–4, 1976.

23. Dennis Chong, *Collective Action and the Civil Rights Movement* (Chicago: University of Chicago Press, 1991), pp. 76–88.

24. Jeffrey Berry, *The Interest Group Society* (New York: HarperCollins, 1989), pp. 16–43, Michael McCann, *Taking Reform Seriously: Perspectives on Public Interest Liberalism* (Ithaca: Cornell University Press, 1986).

25. Philip L. Christenson, "U.S.–South African Economic Relations," in John Barratt and Alfred O. Hero, eds., *The American People and South Africa* (Lexington, Mass.: Lexington Books, 1981), p. 48.

26. Les de Villiers, *In Sight of Surrender: The U.S. Sanctions Campaign Against South Africa, 1946–1993* (New York: Praeger, 1995), pp. 55–56.

27. Christopher Coker, "Collective Bargaining as an International Sanction: The Role of U.S. Corporations in South Africa," *Journal of Modern African Studies* 19, 4 (1981):653–654.

28. Prexy Nesbitt Papers, M 92-335, box 5, Chicago Committee for the Liberation of Mozambique and Angola files, March 16, 1972, State Historical Society, Madison, Wisconsin (hereafter cited as Nesbitt Papers).

29. Minutes, Special Executive Board meeting, American Committee on Africa, October 8, 1970, box 2, folder 27, ACOA Papers.

30. Memo from Eileen Hanson, ACOA field organizer, to Field Staff Evaluations Committee, March 16, 1972, box 2, folder 29, ACOA Papers.

31. Jerry Herman, interview by Billy Nessen, Clarity Film Productions, Berkeley, 1996, p. 8.

32. Ibid., p. 10.

33. Milfred C. Fierce, "Selected Black American Leaders and Organizations and South Africa, 1900–1977," *Journal of Black Studies* 17, 3 (March 1987):305–326.

34. Hill, interview, p. 4.

35. Ibid., p. 5.

36. "Demonstrations at Chrome Arrival," *Southern Africa* 5, 4 (April 1972):15; "ACOA Fact Sheet," American Committee on Africa, December 1972; "Annual Report," American Committee on Africa, January 1972; "Rhodesian Chrome Goes Home," *Southern Africa* 7, 2 (February 1974):22.

37. George Houser, *No One Can Stop the Rain: Glimpses of Africa's Liberation Struggle* (New York: Pilgrim Press, 1989), p. 235.

38. "A Nine Months' Report," Report from the Washington Office on Africa to the American Committee on Africa, October 1968–June 1969, box 2, folder 25, ACOA Papers.

39. Ogene, *Interest Groups*, pp. 147–190.

40. Western Massachusetts Association of Concerned Africanist Scholars, ed., *U.S. Military Involvement in Southern Africa* (Boston: South End Press, 1978).

41. R.B.J. Walker, *One World, Many Worlds: Struggles for a Just World Peace* (Boulder: Lynne Rienner, 1988), pp. 81–115.

42. Memo from Robert Van Lierop, Chicago field office, to Executive Board, American Committee on Africa, February 22, 1972, box 2, folder 29, ACOA Papers.

43. Gerald Bender, James S. Coleman, and Richard L. Sklar, eds., *African Crisis Areas and U.S. Foreign Policy* (Berkeley and Los Angeles: University of California Press, 1986).

44. Gerald Bender, "Kissinger in Angola: Anatomy of Failure," in Rene Lemarchand, ed., *American Policy in Southern Africa: The Stakes and the Stance* (Washington, D.C.: University Press of America, 1981), p. 63.

45. Minutes, Executive Board meeting, American Committee on Africa, September 19, 1974, box 2, folder 32, ACOA Papers.

46. Washington Office on Africa, "Washington Notes on Africa" (Washington, D.C.: Washington Office on Africa, October 1975), p. 3.

47. Hill, interview, p. 7.

5

The Resilience and Revival of Anti-Apartheid Activism, 1976–1983

The previous chapter demonstrated how a series of regime changes in Europe, southern Africa, and the United States converged with paradoxes arising from South Africa's maturing industrial economy to make apartheid a more salient policy problem for Americans. These transitions provided more opportunities for domestic activists to exploit the ensuing vulnerabilities. This chapter focuses on the continuing processes that affected the probability of anti-apartheid mobilization penetrating the policy environment. The approach here contrasts with more traditional stimulus-response explanations of insurgency that view activism primarily as a set of reactions to conventional problems in established policymaking arenas. This analysis instead addresses the long-term development of anti-apartheid activism, its rise and decline in salience, and the ongoing struggle to make the issue appear actionable to the public. It thus stands out from classical approaches that view activism as only reactive.

In particular, this chapter examines how the anti-apartheid movement capitalized on the policy visibility resulting from deepening U.S. entanglement in southern Africa, tracing the way this momentum overcame White House and, later, congressional efforts to reduce the public salience of apartheid. This stage of movement development demonstrates the three major elements of the political process model. The political opportunity structure remained favorable as the intensifying violence in southern Africa penetrated domestic political discourse. Movement organizations consolidated their resources to conduct campaigns that linked corporate and government behavior with support for apartheid. The confidence of activists increased as more thorough media coverage supported their claims that apartheid was the primary agent of the region's conflicts. Opinion polls revealed that significant segments of the public recognized apartheid as a political problem amenable to U.S. intervention.[1]

The Structure of Political Opportunity

It is ironic that 1976, which would have represented the pinnacle of Richard Nixon's political career, began with the former president in virtual exile. Nixon's realist approach toward the region, as embodied in NSSM-39, rationalized confinement of Africa to the foreign policy periphery. Yet by the mid-1970s, the basic assumptions that Africa would remain insulated from great power conflicts and that Africans posed no credible threat to the maintenance of white dominance within the region rapidly disintegrated. These developments also enabled domestic critics of the "Tar Baby" approach to demonstrate that apartheid imposed enormous social and political costs on South Africa and its allies and that U.S. capital and political interests played an integral role in its survival.

South Africa's regional security blanket—consisting of Portugal's colonies, Angola and Mozambique, along with Rhodesia and Namibia, which Pretoria controlled—began to unravel in early 1974. The establishment of the independent Marxist states of Angola and Mozambique, which followed the 1974 collapse of the Portuguese empire, initiated and intensified pressures for change throughout the region.[2]

Congressional adoption of the Clark Amendment in December 1975 severely limited Ford administration efforts to intervene militarily in southern Africa, but other opportunities for involvement in the region soon appeared. The momentum of the Rhodesian civil war shifted in early spring 1976, as a liberation army composed of forces from the Zimbabwe African National Union (ZANU) and the Zimbabwe African Peoples Union (ZAPU), operating from Mozambique's western border, launched a series of strategic attacks against government installations. The escalation of guerrilla warfare crippled Rhodesia's economy, and international opponents of its settler regime redoubled their efforts to further isolate it from external capital and markets. Britain, which had displayed a reluctance to directly challenge Rhodesia since the 1965 Universal Declaration of Independence (UDI), reversed its position by calling for constitutional negotiations between the settler state and liberation representatives and an end to minority rule within two years. Even South Africa acknowledged Rhodesia's vulnerability in reassessing its own security: It was not a question of whether Rhodesia could fall, but when.[3] Pretoria would consequently lose another ally and would have to confront a black invasion from virtually every direction except south.

The transformation of the Rhodesian civil war into a struggle with global power implications suddenly gave Secretary of State Henry Kissinger an opportunity to further certain foreign and domestic objectives by way of southern Africa. Engagement with conflict in Africa conveyed to domestic constituencies the administration's eagerness to challenge Soviet and Cuban intervention and provided a response to conservative criticism leveled by such politicians as former California governor Ronald Reagan, who used the presidential primaries to suggest that Ford was too timid to use force in southern Africa. In late April, Kissinger began a thirteen-day tour of Africa that resembled his previous Mideast shuttle diplomacy. The trip officially centered on conferences with African heads of state about ending the civil war in Rhodesia. Kissinger's initiatives did not rebuild the flagging confidence of the United States in African presidents Kenneth Kaunda of Zambia and Julius Nyerere of Tanzania. The African heads of state noted that the selective character of Washington's denunciation of white supremacy was coupled with its continued presumption that South Africa stabilized the region. Kissinger's mission nevertheless provided an opportunity for him to indirectly concede the failure of NSSM-39 and exhibit a new approach. The secretary of state outlined a new course of action in a speech delivered in Lusaka, Zambia. Kissinger's oratory for the first time included criticism of white minority rule, a professed commitment to the principle of majority rule, and promise to materially assist African states that were trying to solve the region's problems.[4]

But shuttle diplomacy in southern Africa entailed substantial risks because it exposed the administration to further criticism at home and abroad. During a series of primaries in Southern states, Reagan exploited conservative anxieties about racial conflict to revive his faltering campaign. Some analysts attributed Reagan's Texas primary victory to an electorate alarmed that Kissinger's Lusaka speech had sacrificed the interests of Rhodesian whites. More than 100,000 Democrats in Texas, a state troubled with racial tensions over housing and school integration, crossed party lines to vote for Reagan. He also defeated Ford in Alabama and Georgia. By the end of May, Reagan led in the GOP delegate count, 528 to 479, with only six primaries left.[5]

The prospect of diverting public attention from southern Africa further eroded when the Soweto uprisings occurred less than a month after Kissinger's historic African trip. What started as student demonstrations against a requirement that Afrikaans be the medium of instruction erupted into a mass rebellion that threw an international spotlight on the brutality of apartheid, its institutional structure, and regional and global linkages. Soweto, an acronym for the "Southwestern Townships" that housed Johannesburg's black service workers, symbolized the nation's separations—blacks from whites, wealth from poverty, and opportunity from despair. By the mid-1970s, pursuit of the policy of separate development made Soweto and other townships ripe for a revival of black resistance.

The demand for black workers in white urban areas continually undermined the state's elaborate policies mandating racial separation.

Government refusal to accept the permanence of black urban residency led to chronic shortages of housing and schools, which limited the productive capacity of the economy. As South Africa's economy became more thoroughly integrated into the global system, black workers began to experience higher levels of disruption and uncertainty resulting from unemployment and inflation.[6] This fueled the alienation of a generation of black youth that grew up in the rigid post-Sharpeville era. These young people rejected the political complacency of their parents and attached their hopes to the Black Consciousness movement and the liberation struggles in Angola, Mozambique, and Zimbabwe.

Soweto, the community with the largest concentration of urban black youths in South Africa, unexpectedly became the focal point of the nationwide revolt. Unlike the Sharpeville incident of sixteen years earlier, police reaction to unarmed demonstrators in Soweto ignited a wave of nationwide protests that incorporated the general strike and consumer and transportation boycotts as weapons against the state. State repression took a heavy toll: unofficial studies of the revolt concluded that from June to December 1976, over 1,000 persons died, with the number injured exceeding 5,000. Popular resistance endured, attracting international media attention and forcing the government into increased defense spending. The resurgence of a domestic threat introduced reform to official South African political discourse and brought a sense of urgency to negotiations for resolving the crisis in Rhodesia.[7]

Soweto dramatized the Ford administration's pledge to contain radical change in southern Africa and compelled Kissinger to concentrate on the region's problems for the remainder of a critical election year. Less than a week after the Soweto revolt, Kissinger solicited South African prime minister John Vorster's assistance in forcing Rhodesian prime minister Ian Smith to the negotiating table. Kissinger was a reluctant intermediary in fostering dialogue between Vorster, Smith, Kaunda, Nyerere, and Zimbabwe liberation leaders Robert Mugabe and Joshua Nkomo. Kissinger and other international mediators urged the parties to attend a second round of talks in Zurich in early September. Kissinger made several return visits to southern Africa before the presidential elections.[8] Although Kissinger's proposals for a settlement to the Rhodesian conflict proved unacceptable to Zimbabwe nationalists, he succeeded in luring liberation movement representatives and Smith to an October conference in Geneva.

Kissinger's maneuvers on southern Africa carried significant domestic implications, as Ford faced a bitter fight in his bid to stay in the White House. Reagan had capitalized on public uncertainty about the administration's role in Africa to contest Ford's claim on the GOP nomination just weeks before the national party convention. Ford eventually won the nomination in a close race, but the ruptures that Reagan created between party moderates and conservatives reinforced a sense of urgency in expanding the incumbent's electoral base. Against this backdrop of party division and declining popular support, Kissinger attempted to cultivate a black foreign policy constituency for the president by initiating a series of meetings with civil rights groups. Using tactics reminiscent of John F. Kennedy's surrogate use of Africa in the 1960 campaign as a way of enticing black voters,[9] Kissinger delivered major speeches on Africa policy to the National Urban League and the Philadelphia-based Opportunities Industries Corporation and arranged private meetings with black leaders such as Reverend Jesse Jackson and Manhattan borough president Percy Sutton. Just as the administration's belated arrival on the southern Africa scene had handicapped its efforts to address the complexities of the region, however, its appeals to black Americans lagged behind those made by Democratic candidate Jimmy Carter.

The electoral salience of southern Africa's racial conflicts for the U.S. black constituency proved auspicious for Carter. Running as an outsider to the Washington establishment, the one-term Georgia governor did not develop substantial black support outside Georgia until midway through the primaries. The turning point came in the Florida primary as black voters mobilized to derail the campaign of former Alabama governor and arch-segregationist George Wallace. Carter defeated Wallace, and the overwhelming support Carter received from black voters led to refinements in his campaign strategy for appealing to the African-American electorate.[10] Carter received endorsements from black Southern politicians such as Congressman Andrew Young and Martin Luther King Sr., father of the slain civil rights activist, which allowed him to strengthen his claim on civil rights movement rhetoric. A short-term strategy thus put Carter in position to take advantage of three critical elements that could influence election outcomes: the enlargement of the black electorate as a result of the Voting Rights Act; growth of black interest in foreign affairs; and Kissinger's failure to reduce racial tensions in southern Africa.

The delayed development of Carter's foreign policy positions exhibited a pattern similar to his response to black voters. As a businessman and governor of Georgia, Carter had had little experience in foreign affairs before he was recruited into David Rockefeller's Trilateral Commission in 1973. It was among this network of liberal internationalist corporate executives and bankers that much of Carter's generalist foreign policy education took place. In the wake of Kissinger's "realist" miscalculations, Carter's eagerness to view the emerging global community as amenable to American morality and values captured the attention of critics of U.S. policies in southern Africa. Carter's view, in contrast to the

Republican Party's anxiety about race, embraced the civil rights experience and black community interest in foreign affairs for use as tools to sharpen America's focus on Africa. "It would be a great help to this nation if people in public life were to be made aware of the problems of Africa through a significant Black interest in Africa," he asserted. "Americans might not have made the mistakes we made in Vietnam had there been an articulate Vietnamese minority in our midst."[11]

South Africa's eroding regional security perimeter, the Soweto rebellion, and the enhanced visibility of foreign capital encouraged anti-apartheid activism in the United States. From 1975 to 1977, South Africa experienced its worst economic recession since the 1930s, as its gross domestic product (GDP) sank from an average growth of 11.8 percent in 1964–1974 to zero in 1977.[12] Similarly, the inflation rate soared from 3.3 percent in 1970 to 11 percent in 1977. When the recession combined with rapid decline in foreign investment after Soweto and endangered major infrastructure development plans, the state borrowed more from foreign banks and imposed limitations on foreign capital repatriation.

The uncertainty of South Africa's investment climate widened domestic exposure to four key aspects of the U.S. relationship to apartheid. First, American investments in South Africa had doubled between 1970 and 1976, rising to $1.67 billion, or nearly 40 percent of all U.S. dollars in Africa. Second, American reliance on South African minerals paralleled developments in vital sectors of the domestic economy. The demand for platinum-group minerals used to produce unleaded fuels and catalytic converters, for example, escalated in response to the Clean Air Act of 1974. Manufacturers of stainless steel, heat-resistant parts for jet engines, and computer components also came to depend upon strategic minerals from South Africa and its neighbors. Third, American capital demonstrated a propensity to adjust to fluctuations in the South African political economy. As the investment-risk assessment of South Africa shifted from the "acceptable" to "moderate" category after Soweto, banks began curtailing long-term loans to South Africa in favor of short-term, high-interest credits. Finally, the U.S. role as intermediary in securing International Monetary Fund credits for South Africa expanded. The IMF approved the first credit of $366 million in March 1976 and a second credit of $98 million ten months later. The Senate Subcommittee on African Affairs in 1976 investigated these loans and other corporate activities in South Africa.[13]

The political winds of change in southern Africa had penetrated the 1976 presidential election and introduced significant elements of the anti-apartheid movement's agenda into policy discussion. During the campaign, Carter criticized the reactive character of the Ford administration's dealings with southern Africa and emphasized the centrality of human rights as a standard for assessing commitments abroad. After the election, Carter outlined plans to develop a more restrained and democratic foreign policy.[14]

The Liberal Ascent Under Carter

The reformulation of African strategies consonant with these visions prompted Carter to assemble a team of policymakers experienced in African affairs and sensitive to the issue of majority rule in southern Africa. These appointments, which included Anthony Lake (director of policy planning at the State Department), Ruth Schacter Morgenthau (UNESCO adviser), Goler Butcher (director of the Africa section of the Agency for International Development), Donald McHenry (deputy ambassador to the UN), Richard Moose (assistant secretary of state for African affairs), and Andrew Young (ambassador to the UN), also provided bridges to two previously underrepresented foreign policy constituencies: professional Africanists and black Americans. Young, the former civil rights activist and Georgia congressman, assumed the most visible role on southern African issues. Young echoed Carter's optimism: The triumph over racial segregation at home had endowed the administration with expertise for dealing with southern Africa's racial strife. "I think our country has established through our own experience in race relationships, and particularly in the South, an understanding of this very sensitive issue of black and white people within the same community," he declared. "With the special knowledge in our country, I think we might be a help in Africa."[15]

The new administration's flurry of activity on southern Africa during its first six months seemingly indicated that human rights and racial equality had acquired higher levels of significance in U.S. foreign policy. Carter's inaugural address emphasized these concerns as the cornerstone of America's new relationship with the international community. The first in a series of high-profile maneuvers accenting this theme in the administration's approach to southern Africa unfolded in May, when Vice President Walter Mondale met with Prime Minister Vorster in Geneva. The vice president warned that Pretoria's failure to implement meaningful reforms and expand political participation would worsen relations with the United States. Although Mondale did not offer a blueprint for reform, he implied that nothing less than "one man, one vote" would suffice.[16] Secretary of State Cyrus Vance elaborated on administration objectives in a July speech at the NAACP's annual meeting. Vance maintained that Carter's promotion of racial justice in southern Africa reflected his long-term objectives and was not merely a reaction to Soviet and Cuban involvement in Africa.[17] None of these highly publicized events signaled fundamental policy shifts, but all contributed to restoring credibility with selective constituencies at home and abroad.

These episodes distinguished Carter's approach toward southern Africa from that of his predecessor, yet they disguised the administration's limited comprehension of the region and its anxiety about how impending change would occur. One of the most revealing moments of this uneasiness occurred when Ambassador Young toured Africa in late May 1977. Young's trip generated substantial media comment because he embodied the black electorate's Africa concerns and could easily articulate their antagonism toward U.S. complicity with white colonial regimes. Young's designation of domestic civil rights strategies as the appropriate mechanisms for contesting racial inequality angered many Africans, however. He lectured Soweto students on the power of nonviolent protests and boycotts as weapons against apartheid, while affirming the priority of the economic arena as a catalyst for political change. Contrary to conventional wisdom, Young argued that the "private sector began to move toward desegregation in the South as early as 1960–61, while Congress didn't get around to the Civil Rights Act until 1964."[18] Young's brief for free enterprise belied his "militancy" and underlined the Carter administration's aversion to disturbing vital economic and strategic interests.

Carter proved less adept at altering the substance of relations with South Africa than in introducing new rhetoric and symbols into policy discourse. Human rights and racial equality remained lofty ideals, but officials clearly believed that corporate capital was the most effective mechanism for promoting change in South Africa. This faith, ironically, combined with the uncertainty after Soweto, furnished the carrot and stick that spurred U.S. businesses to modify their image and relationships with the apartheid system.[19]

Corporations initiated a series of high visibility projects in 1977. In a new spirit of corporate activism, 130 American companies established a chamber of commerce in Johannesburg in November. One of the chamber's first ventures involved raising nearly $3 million for the construction of a Soweto high school and $.5 million more for its annual operating costs.[20] The high school addressed a major deficiency of the apartheid bureaucratic apparatus and enabled U.S. businesses to challenge state policies under the guise of promoting economic efficiency. The chamber also lobbied South African regulatory bodies for workplace reforms.

A more ambitious intervention proposal by Leon Sullivan, a black minister from Philadelphia who served on the board of directors of General Motors, created new expectations of business as an agent of change. Sullivan, director of Opportunities Industries Corporation, a program that linked the corporate community and inner-city residents through job training, announced a six-point code of corporate conduct in 1977. The so-called Sullivan Principles (also called the Sullivan Code), included:

1. Non-segregation of the races in all eating, comfort, locker rooms, and work facilities.
2. Equal and fair employment practices for all employees.
3. Equal pay for all employees doing equal or comparable work for the same period of time.
4. Initiation and development of training programs that will prepare blacks, Coloureds, and Asians in substantial numbers for supervisory, administrative, clerical and technical jobs.
5. Increasing the number of blacks, Coloureds, and Asians in management and supervisory positions.
6. Improving the quality of employees' lives outside the work environment in such areas as housing, transportation, and schooling, recreating, and health facilities.[21]

Twelve firms—American Cyanamid, Burroughs, Caltex Petroleum, Citicorp, Ford, General Motors, IBM, International Harvester, 3M, Mobil, Otis Elevator, and Union Carbide—immediately adopted the Sullivan Principles, and by the end of the year, fifty-four had signed on. Over the next two years, 135 of the 300 U.S. companies in South Africa had endorsed the code. The Carter administration supported the Sullivan Principles but refused to make them mandatory. Domestic opponents of the codes saw them as having little effect on the fundamental structure of apartheid, since American firms employed only 1 percent of all South Africa workers and corporate codes of conduct left intact vast domains of legal segregation practiced in housing, citizenship, and voting rights. Critics such as the NAACP, the AFL-CIO, and TransAfrica argued that apartheid warranted destruction, not reform and that national corporations should withdraw completely from South Africa.[22]

As the Carter administration and business interests recognized South African political fragility, key factions in Congress exploited this opening to advocate policy liberalization. In early 1977, the House reconvened the Subcommittee on Africa, which began an investigation of the impact of sanctions against Rhodesia, nuclear ties to South Africa, Pretoria's policies on internal migration, and its repressive institutions. Other House subcommittees conducting hearings on policy toward southern Africa included the Subcommittee on Science, Research, and Technology, which explored the effects of southern African political instability on procurement of strategic minerals; the Subcommittee on International Trade, Investment, and Monetary Policy, which examined Export-Import Bank policies and the South African economy; and the Subcommittee on International Organizations, which inquired into Pretoria's human rights record. The peak of executive-legislative branch cooperation on southern African took place when Congress, at the request of the administration, repealed the Byrd Amendment, which had allowed national companies to import Rhodesian chromium in violation of UN sanctions. Revocation of the sanctions loophole removed one of the last excuses available to business and lobbyists claiming legitimacy for the Smith government. Most important, the repeal of the Byrd Amendment introduced the possibility that South Africa could be subjected to the same discipline as Rhodesia.

High-profile reform measures by the federal government and corporations captured Pretoria's attention but did not substantially alter its violent pursuit of separate racial development. Throughout the late 1970s, the Vorster government announced reforms that seemingly abandoned long-term plans to relocate blacks away from white urban areas to their own "homelands." Presented as a way to transfer small amounts of administrative authority to selected black patrons of the state, these reforms did nothing to modify the racialized political hierarchy. The softening of selected state policies on migration coincided with increased bannings or house arrest of dissidents and controls on political dissent. The arrest and murder of BCM leader Steve Biko while in police custody in fall 1977 generated additional surges of international attention. Less than a month after Biko's death, the state banned over twenty African or multiracial organizations, arrested forty black political leaders, shut down two leading African newspapers, arrested their editors, and banned seven white opposition figures.

By the end of 1977, the economy exhibited signs of rebounding from a prolonged recession. This resulted from infusions of foreign capital, increased retention of earnings from foreign investment, and refinements in the capacity to evade international sanctions. The government received a vote of confidence from the white electorate in a referendum that strengthened its hand against internal opposition and foreign pressures to liberalize.

South Africa's defiance of international expectations corresponded to significant alterations in the U.S. policymaking environment after the 1978 midterm elections. The Carter administration exhibited this shift as a series of international conflicts—the Cuban presence in Angola, the Shaba insurrection against the Mobutu government in Zaire, the overthrow of the shah of Iran, and the Soviet invasion of Afghanistan—reinvigorated anticommunist frameworks for interpreting political instability. The regionalists within the administration—those who rejected an exclusive East-West outlook—gained some degree of influence during the early forays into southern Africa. The globalists, however, led by national security adviser Zbigniew Brzezinski, reasserted the traditional predisposition to view African issues through the lens of U.S.-Soviet strategic relations.[23] Carter fired Andrew Young in late 1979, after the UN ambassador admitted that he had held an unauthorized meeting with representatives of the Palestine Liberation Organization. Prospects for a reformed policy toward southern Africa declined further with the loss of congressional liberals such as Dick Clark in 1978,[24] Charles C. Diggs in 1979, and George McGovern in 1980.

The period dating from the termination of U.S. military involvement in Southeast Asia in mid-1975 through Carter's first year in office represented a period of liberal ascendancy in southern African affairs. Congress often displayed a willingness to challenge presidential dominance and an eagerness to explore alternative visions of America's relationship with the world. This milieu proved somewhat short-lived and did not include a fundamental redefinition of foreign policy. Carter's policies for the most part reflected a fundamental conservatism, caution, and tolerance for discredited notions about colonialism and race. As international problems grew more complex, few policy officials relinquished Cold War constructions of the dilemmas confronting the developing world.

Business-Driven Policy in the Reagan Years

Ronald Reagan completely rejected Carter's flirtation with openness toward the global community. From Reagan's perspective, responsibility for the turmoil in the region rested with the Soviet Union rather than with the institutional relics of racism and colonialism. In his attack on Ford's foreign policy the previous year, Reagan had charged Kissinger with being too soft on the Soviets, giving away the Panama Canal, and sidestepping the use of military force. Reagan's critique of Carter unfolded in 1977 while the administration conducted a series of sensitive discussions with South Africa about racial reform. Reagan declared that U.S. concern with human rights in southern Africa "clouds our ability to see this international danger [Soviet interests] to the Western world."[25] Reagan avoided comment on Africa during the 1980 campaign, but his team of advisers reflected the same static view of the region. The advisers included veteran diplomat Ernest Lefever; Richard Allen, who had been Nixon's special envoy to the Portuguese dictatorship; and academics such as Hoover Institution historian Peter Duignan, who favored "détente" with South Africa; and Georgetown University political scientists Jeane Kirkpatrick and Chester Crocker.[26]

After defeating Carter in 1980, Reagan initiated a costly military buildup designed to reassert U.S. hegemony and contain Soviet influence.

Reagan, maintaining that any Soviet gain was a U.S. loss, advocated promoting America's geopolitical interests through a strong South Africa, even at the cost of overlooking its internal policies and aggression toward its neighbors. Kirkpatrick, Reagan's ambassador to the UN, believed that the United States could not work with Marxist states, which she labeled totalitarian. Yet South Africa, which she characterized as an authoritarian regime, presented no such problem: She claimed that "racist dictatorship is not as bad as Marxist dictatorship."[27]

Crocker, a former member of Kissinger's national security staff, became assistant secretary of state for Africa and emerged as the architect of an administration policy toward South Africa referred to as "constructive engagement." Constructive engagement involved ongoing conversations and cooperation with the minority regime. He emphasized gradual evolution toward democracy, which could only be realized with white South African assistance. The belief that majority rule would necessarily entail bloodshed and disorder lay embedded in this notion. Crocker urged Americans to consider the needs and insecurities of whites before they called for a rapid end to apartheid. In contrast to the Carter administration's mild reproof, Crocker's approach toward South Africa seemed downright conciliatory.[28]

Viewing South Africa as a "modernizing autocracy," the administration anticipated expansion of the republic's role in the Western defense system.[29] Reagan officials relied upon a set of perspectives on race relations thoroughly discredited in the United States, as well as in other Western societies. From Reagan's standpoint, the existence of a system of racial discrimination was insufficient evidence to call for dismantling apartheid. Reagan shared Nixon's relaxed stance of a decade earlier toward the settler states. He viewed white South Africa as a citadel of stability and defender of Western values and institutions. When CBS reporter Walter Cronkite asked about his attitude toward applying sanctions to South Africa, Reagan replied: "Can we abandon a country that has stood by us in every war we've ever fought, a country that strategically is essential to the free world in its production of minerals we all must have and so forth?"[30] Reagan's zealous endorsement of this relationship glossed over the pro-Nazi sympathies of South Africa's ruling National Party, which, though out of power during World War II, had opposed the Grand Alliance.

The Reagan administration embarked upon a series of measures designed to normalize relations with South Africa. It urged the Republican-dominated Senate to repeal the Clark Amendment, which restricted support to anti-Marxist guerrillas in Angola. It softened Carter-era trade restrictions, enabling South Africa to purchase dual-purpose equipment for civilian use, such as aircraft and computers, but easily adaptable

Chester Crocker, assistant secretary of state and architect of Reagan's "constructive engagement" policy toward South Africa. As Reagan's point man on Africa, Crocker became a magnet for critics of administration policy in the mid-1980s.

SOURCE: *Africa News*, April 8, 1985.

for military and security purposes. The U.S. Commerce Department opened a trade promotion office in Johannesburg, while South Africa opened new consulates in Denver, Cleveland, and Seattle. Reagan officials also urged IMF approval of Pretoria's application for a $1.1 billion loan.[31]

White House approaches to Pretoria echoed strategies chosen by U.S. businesses. In the early 1980s, more than 6,000 American firms conducted business in South Africa, with significant investments in the extractive industries. Other sectors of the economy benefited from the U.S. corporate presence. The fast-food industry, including companies such as Pizza Hut and Kentucky Fried Chicken, entered the South African market in 1982 using local franchisees. Extended air travel between the two countries reflected increased trade. During the same year, South African Airways began weekly flights to Houston to supplement its regularly scheduled flights from Johannesburg to New York. For a moment, it seemed that the boom years of the early 1970s had returned.

Reagan's election created an aura of new possibilities for South Africa. The National Party government was in accord with the newly elected president's suspicion of the Soviet Union, his faith in Western institutions and market-based economics as the primary agents of political change, and his aggressive endorsement of militarily reversing the gains of Marxist states. Apart from ideological compatibility, Pretoria saw the United States as a key supporter for its claim to be a valid member of the Western alliance.[32]

South African fears about regional security escalated as Zimbabwe gained its independence in 1979 and in the next year became the third Marxist government in southern Africa. Pretoria's uneasiness stemmed from the potential of these states to intensify international pressures against it and to collaborate with the African National Congress to politically mobilize South African blacks. For more than a decade, the South African military regularly launched air and ground assaults on its neighbors. These attacks, ostensibly aimed at ANC rebels, provided support for antigovernment forces: UNITA in Angola, and the Resistencia Nacional Moçambicana (RENAMO) in Mozambique.[33] The Reagan administration justified these actions as defensive, using its veto against UN resolutions condemning Pretoria. Deputy secretary of state William Clark best characterized the first stage of the Reagan years in a speech given in South Africa: "Let this be the beginning of mutual trust and confidence between the United States and South Africa, old friends, like Minister Botha, who are getting together again."[34]

Despite the optimism that accompanied rejuvenation of Pretoria's friendship with Washington, South Africa's economy began to display signs of instability that called into question the post-Soweto recovery. A brief rise in the price of gold and adept management of obstacles posed by limited oil and arms embargoes appeared to make the economy sufficiently robust to enable the state to weather further disruptions in pursuit of its "total strategy" for maintaining white supremacy.[35] The total strategy was based on the assumption that state co-optation of business reformers and moderate black leaders could create the economic and political conditions necessary to cushion South Africa against external marketplace fluctuations. Yet by late 1981, as gold prices resumed their downward trend, signs of a deeper recession surfaced as the GDP fell to 4 percent, nearly one-half its rate the previous year. The balance of trade similarly sank from a $7-billion surplus in 1980 to a $1-billion deficit in 1981. These trends exposed the fragility of South Africa's economy and its political uncertainty.

Economic fluctuation induced South African business leaders to solicit reform of the apartheid system. They at first called for such efficiency measures as reduction in governmental controls and better transportation and training for black workers. As the economic boom-and-bust cycles revealed major structural weaknesses resistant to the effects of increased foreign investment or state controls, however, business leaders pushed for more fundamental political and economic changes. The Urban Foundation, a major business group formed in the aftermath of the Soweto uprisings, began submitting reform proposals in 1978 and continued to lobby for a greater voice in national planning. The state responded by initiating a series of meetings, dubbed the Carleton Conference, to incorporate business recommendations into policymaking.[36]

A confidential report by the South African Foundation in 1980 added urgency to business recommendations regarding the disruptive potential of foreign capital flight. The report acknowledged the possibility of disturbances emanating from American anti-apartheid group pressures on U.S. firms operating in South Africa. Several corporate officials admitted that responding to sanctions and divestment measures consumed more than 30 percent of their time.[37] Although profits in South Africa remained high, foreign companies began to reassess the long-term prospects for their investments. While some firms joined in campaigns to lobby the state for reforms, others began to restructure their investments in South Africa, using strategies such as selling stock to local companies, shifting investments from loans to credits, and outright disinvestment. European enterprises in particular, energized by anti-apartheid movements back home, adopted plans to reduce or curtail their spending in South Africa.

By early 1983 the American business community's confidence in the South African economy began to waiver. Frequently erratic economic conditions suggested that neither increasing expenditures nor relying on controls improvised by the South African state could reduce the need for fundamental change throughout South African society. Black union membership grew steadily in the early 1970s and by the end of the decade had achieved official recognition. As mobilization around work issues invariably spilled over into the domain of state restrictions on race, industry experienced increases in labor unrest. Political ferment increased when the government created a new constitution establishing a parliament for whites, a separate one for Coloureds and Indians, but none for Africans. Protest activity galvanized in 1983 with the formation of the United Democratic Front (UDF), a coalition of workers, students, African, colored, and white opponents of the state. Ever-stricter governmental controls, mounting resistance, and rising worldwide debate about apartheid drove up the costs of doing business in South Africa.

For most of Reagan's first term, Crocker and the Republican-controlled Senate effectively blocked direct congressional challenges to standard policy by steering discussion away from the cruelties of apartheid, instead characterizing southern African turmoil as incited by the Soviets. As regional conditions deteriorated, however, Congress surfaced as a focal point for challenging the administration and promoting policies more compatible with the changing realities of southern Africa. Several administration maneuvers backfired and supplied critics with key points of access into policy debates.

The first notable domestic uproar against constructive engagement resulted from Ambassador Kirkpatrick's 1981 secret meeting with five high-ranking South African military intelligence officers. The Congressional Black Caucus, calling attention to Andrew Young's firing two years earlier for having met with unauthorized representatives of the Palestine Liberation Organization, demanded that Reagan take similar action. He declined to do so. After Kirkpatrick's veto of a UN Security Council vote condemning South Africa's invasion of Angola, the CBC scored the administration's double standard on human rights violation. CBC protests made little policy impact but kept morality issues on the table.

Next, in spring 1982, the administration announced its intention to soften the ban on exports to the South African police and military. The House Committee on Foreign Affairs voted to reimpose export controls. Four senators—Massachusetts Democrats Paul Tsongas and Edward Kennedy and Republican conservatives Rudy Boschwitz of Minnesota and Larry Pressler of South Dakota—wrote legislation opposing any relaxation of the ban. Neither of these measures gained the necessary votes to overrule the president, but they raised public questions about complicity with a conspicuous violator of human rights.[38]

Despite Charles Diggs's abrupt departure in 1979 due to a political scandal, his successor, Stephen J. Solarz of New York, preserved the Subcommittee on Africa's role as a critical arena for challenging administration policy. As the Carter administration retreated from anti-apartheid, the subcommittee reviewed U.S. policy commitments. "We may have another Iran on our hands," Solarz declared. "For what seemed good reasons at the time, we became identified with a Government which now appears to have lost the support of its own people, and which may not survive no matter what we are likely to do for it."[39]

Solarz also used hearings to illustrate how support for anticommunist African authoritarian leaders such as Mobutu in Zaire undermined basic human rights and tarnished the American image in Africa. Solarz left the Subcommittee on Africa in 1981 to become chair of the Subcommittee on Asia. His successor, Michigan representative Howard Wolpe, brought impressive credentials as a professional Africanist with an advanced degree in African studies, as did the two top staff members of the subcommittee, Anne Forrester Holloway and Stephen F. Weissman.[40]

Congress, acting as a kind of guardian of the public trust, can direct public attention to aspects of administration policy that would otherwise go unnoticed. The skills concentrated in the subcommittee thus assured professional Africanists of greater access to the congressional policymaking process. Congressional expertise can effectively disrupt a popular president's honeymoon with the supportive members of his own party, the media, and the attentive public. Legislative critiques of administration policy could lay it bare more effectively than could a small number of dissident voices. Under Wolpe's leadership, the subcommittee maintained a strong interest in oversight of policy toward southern Africa. As Table 5.1 indicates, the subcommittee became a major site in the policy arena for linking critics of administration policy, professional Africanists, and anti-apartheid groups at critical stages as the apartheid regime unraveled.

By the late 1970s, other sources in Congress had become associated with anti-apartheid sentiments. The 1979 formation of the Ad Hoc

TABLE 5.1　Witness Affiliation, Subcommittee on Africa Hearings, 1959–1988

Year	No. of Hearings	Executive Branch	Members of Congress	Corporate	Interest Groups	Academics
1959–1960	2	2	–	–	–	–
1961–1962	1	1	–	11	11	–
1963–1964	2	3	–	–	–	–
1965–1966	1	8	1	2	11	11
1967–1968	–	–	–	–	–	–
1969–1970	2	7	1	2	1	4
1971–1972	7	4	–	3	18	3
1973–1974	9	2	–	–	17	4
1975–1976	Congressional reorganization abolishes geographic region committees and reestablishes hearings under the aegis of the International Relations Committee					
1977–1978	13	7	4	–	9	7
1979–1980	12	15	5	14	39	40
1981–1982	11	1	5	–	9	8
1983–1984	6	4	5	2	14	4
1985–1986	4	31	8	4	9	2
1987–1988	1	6	1	–	6	6

SOURCE: *Monthly Catalog of United States Government Publications* (Washington, D.C.: 1958–1970); *Congressional Information Service Index to Publications of the United States Congress* (Washington, D.C.: 1970–1988).

Monitoring Group on Southern Africa, a bipartisan group from both houses of Congress, helped coordinate policy responses and attempted to neutralize the impact of conservative gains in the 1978 midterm elections. Midway through Reagan's first term, other subcommittees such as the Subcommittees on International Economic Policy and Trade; Fiscal Affairs and Public Health; Human Rights and International Organization; and Financial Institution Supervision, Regulation, and Insurance had taken up African issues.[41]

Conclusion

The dilemma that southern Africa posed for policymakers from 1976 to 1983 revealed not only the consequences of the Nixon administration's neglect but also how the institutional framework for dealing with African issues by both Republican and Democratic administrations retained a limited view that perpetually put it at odds with the dynamics of the region. In spite of major political changes during this period, the presidency remained wedded to an anachronistic Cold War view of southern Africa even when that perspective undermined the national interest. In a relatively short time, southern African resistance had weakened assumptions about the permanence of great power control of the area and led to new dimensions of power in the foreign policymaking process. When public debate invited comparisons with Southeast Asia, glimpses of the human costs of complicity with a repressive society were revealed.

Notes

1. Deborah Durfee Barron and John Immerwahr, "The Public Views South Africa: Pathways Through a Gathering Storm," *Public Opinion* 2 (January–February 1979):54–59.

2. George Shepherd, *Anti-Apartheid: Transnational Conflict and Western Policy in the Liberation of South Africa* (Westport, Conn.: Greenwood Press, 1977).

3. Colin Legum, *Southern Africa: Year of the Whirlwind* (New York: African Publishing Company, 1977), p. 14; Carol B. Thompson, *Challenge of Imperialism: The Frontline States in the Liberation of Zimbabwe* (Boulder: Westview Press, 1985).

4. Henry A. Kissinger, "United States Policy on Southern Africa," *Department of State Bulletin* 74, 1927 (May 31, 1976):672–679.

5. In January 1974, South African lobbyists operating in the United States included Governor Reagan, among those in a group of national leaders viewed as sympathetic to whites in southern Africa. Les de Villiers, *In Sight of Surrender: The U.S. Sanctions Campaign Against South Africa, 1946–1993* (New York: Praeger, 1995), p. 37; John Robert Greene, *The Presidency of Gerald R. Ford* (Lawrence: University of Kansas Press, 1994), p. 167; James P. Sterba, "Reagan Victor over Ford by Huge Margin in Texas," *New York Times*, May 2, 1976.

6. Darryl Thomas and William G. Martin, "South Africa's Economic Trajectory: South African Crisis or World Economic Crisis?" in Sergio Vieira, William G. Martin, and Immanuel Wallerstein, eds., *How Fast the Wind: Southern Africa, 1975–2000* (Trenton, N.J.: Africa World Press, 1992), pp. 165–196.

7. Robert Price, *The Apartheid State in Crisis, 1975–1990* (New York: Oxford University Press, 1991), p. 48; William Minter, *King Solomon's Mines Revisited: Western Interests and the Burdened History of Southern Africa* (New York: Basic Books, 1986), pp. 277–278.

8. Kevin Danaher, *The Political Economy of U.S. Policy Toward South Africa* (Boulder: Westview Press, 1985), pp. 122–123.

9. Richard D. Mahoney, *JFK: Ordeal in Africa* (New York: Oxford University Press, 1983), pp. 30–31.

10. Ronald W. Walters, *Black Presidential Politics in America: A Strategic Approach* (Albany: SUNY Press, 1988), pp. 33–34.

11. "Election '76: Jimmy Carter on Africa," *Africa Report* 21, 3 (May–June 1976):18–20.

12. Republic of South Africa, Bureau of Statistics, *Statistical Data*, September 1978, pp. 96–99.

13. U.S. Department of Commerce, Bureau of the Census, *Statistical Abstract of the United States*, 1970–1984; U.S. Congress, House, Committee on Interior and Insular Affairs, *Sub-Saharan Africa: Its Role in Critical Mineral Needs of the Western World. Hearings*, 96th Cong., 2d sess., July 1980; "Apartheid: South African Credit Bar," *New York Times*, April 22, 1978; Desaix Myers III, with Kenneth Propp, David Hauck, and David M. Liff, *U.S. Business in South Africa: The Economic, Political, and Moral Issues* (Bloomington: Indiana University Press, 1980), pp. 42–43; U.S. Congress, Senate, Committee on Foreign Relations, Subcommittee on African Affairs, *South Africa—U.S. Policy and the Role of U.S. Corporations. Hearings.* 94th Cong., 2d sess., 1976.

14. U.S. President, *Public Papers of the Presidents of the United States, Jimmy Carter*, vol. 2 (1977), pp. 957–962.

15. Danaher, *Political Economy of U.S. Policy*, p. 161; H. E. Newsum and Olayiwola Abegunrin, *United States Foreign Policy Towards Southern Africa: Andrew Young and Beyond* (New York: St. Martin's Press, 1987).

16. Study Commission on United States Policy Toward Southern Africa, *South Africa: Time Running Out* (Berkeley and Los Angeles: University of California Press, 1986), p. 358.

17. Cyrus Vance, "U.S. Policy Toward Africa," Department of State, Bureau of Public Affairs (July 1, 1977), p. 2.

18. U.S. Congress, Committee on Foreign Affairs, Subcommittee on African Affairs, *Ambassador Young's African Trip. Hearings*, 95th Cong., 1st sess., June 6, 1977, pp 6–7.

19. Myers et al., *U.S. Business in South Africa*, p. 95.

20. Ibid., p. 75; Miriam Lacob, "Black Reactions to Reagan," *Africa Report* 27, 4 (July–August 1982):48–51.

21. David Hauck, Meg Voorhes, and Glenn Goldberg, *Two Decades of Debate: The Controversy over U.S. Companies in South Africa* (Washington, D.C.: Investor Responsibility Research Center, 1983), p. 155.

22. Myers et al., *U.S. Business in South Africa*, p. 93; Elizabeth Schmidt, *Decoding Corporate Camouflage: U.S. Business Support for Apartheid* (Washington, D.C.: Institute for Policy Studies, 1980); George Houser, *No One Can Stop the Rain: Glimpses of Africa's Liberation Struggle* (New York: Pilgrim Press, 1989), p. 350.

23. Zbigniew Brzezinski, *Power and Principle: Memoirs of the National Security Advisor, 1977–1981* (New York: Farrar, Straus, Giroux, 1983).

24. Clark's opponent Roger Culver received substantial campaign funds from the South Africa Foundation, which, it was later revealed, participated in a corrupt influence-peddling scheme known as Muldergate. Minter, *King Solomon's Mines Revisited*, p. 300.

25. "Reagan Critical of Carter on Rights," *New York Times,* June 10, 1977.

26. Richard Deutsch, "Reagan's African Perspectives," *Africa Report* (July–August 1980):4–7.

27. Robert Fatton, "The Reagan Foreign Policy Toward South Africa: The Ideology of a New Cold War," *African Studies Review* 27, 1 (March 1984):57–58; "Africa: Certainly Not Neglected," *Economist* 278, 7178 (March 28, 1981), p. 24.

28. Chester Crocker, *High Noon in Southern Africa: Making Peace in a Rough Neighborhood* (New York: W. W. Norton, 1992); Chester Crocker, "South Africa: Strategy for Change," *Foreign Affairs* 59, 2 (Winter 1980–1981):323–351.

29. Crocker, "South Africa: Strategy for Change," p. 337; Lefever, nominated to become head of the Human Rights Division at the Department of State, testified in House Subcommittee on Africa hearings in 1979 that the United States should not be concerned with South Africa's racial policies but should accept that nation as a full-fledged partner in the struggle against communism. U.S. President, *Public Papers of the President, Ronald Reagan* (1981), pp. 196–197.

30. Pauline Baker, *The United States and South Africa: The Reagan Years* (New York: Ford Foundation and Foreign Policy Association, 1989), p. 25.

31. Richard W. Hull, *American Enterprise in South Africa* (New York: New York University Press, 1990), p. 319.

32. Baker, *The United States and South Africa*, p. 25.

33. William Minter, *Apartheid's Contras: An Inquiry into the Roots of War in Angola and Mozambique* (London: Zed Press, 1994); Christine Sylvester, *Zimbabwe: The Terrain of Contradictory Development* (Boulder: Westview Press, 1991).

34. Joseph Lelyveld, "U.S. Envoy Ends Talk with Botha on the Independence of Namibia," *New York Times,* June 12, 1981.

35. Sergio Vieira and Thomas Ohlson, "The Region as a Zone of Geostrategical Struggle," in Vieira, Martin, and Wallerstein, *How Fast the Wind*, pp. 204–207.

36. Price, *The Apartheid State in Crisis*, pp. 88–90.

37. "South Africa's Foot-Dragging Vexes U.S. Companies," *Business Week* 2659 (October 20, 1980), pp. 56–58.

38. "House Foreign Affairs Committee Reimposes Export Controls on South Africa," *Congressional Quarterly Weekly Report* 40, 21 (May 22, 1982):1184; "Four Senators Introduce Legislation Objecting to Reagan's March 1 Decision," *Congressional Quarterly Weekly Report* 40, 15 (April 10, 1982):842.

39. U.S. House, Committee on Foreign Affairs, Subcommittee on Africa, *Foreign Assistance Legislation for Fiscal Years 1980–81* (Part 6), *Economic and Military Assis-*

tance Programs in Africa. Hearings and Markup, February 13, 14, 21, 22, 27, 28; March 5, 6, 7, 12, 1979, 96th Cong., 1st sess., pp. 351–352.

40. Anne Forrester Holloway, "Congressional Initiatives on South Africa," in Gerald J. Bender, James S. Coleman, and Richard L. Sklar, eds., *African Crisis Areas and U.S. Foreign Policy* (Berkeley and Los Angeles: University of California Press, 1986), pp. 89–94; Stephen F. Weissman, *American Foreign Policy in the Congo, 1960–1964* (Ithaca: Cornell University Press, 1974).

41. Hearings focused on U.S. corporate activities in South Africa, controls on exports to South Africa, human rights in South Africa, and the impact of divestment from South Africa on the U.S. economy. Subcommittee on Africa and Subcommittee on International Economic Policy and Trade, *U.S. Corporate Activities in South Africa, Hearings,* September 24 and October 15, 22, 1981, May 18 and June 10, 1982, 97th Cong., 2d sess.; Subcommittee on Fiscal Affairs and Public Health, *South Africa Divestment,* January 31 and February 7, 1984, 98th Cong., 2d sess.; Subcommittee on Human Rights and Subcommittee on International Organizations, *Implementation of Congressionally Mandated Human Rights Provisions,* November 5, 17 and December 10, 1981, and February 23 and March 9, 17, 1982, 98th Congress, 2d Session; Banking, Finance, and Urban Affairs Committee, Subcommittee on Financial Institutions, Supervision, Regulation and Insurance, *South African Restrictions,* June 8, 1983, 98th Cong., 1st sess.

6

Organizational Growth: New Directions and Strategies

It was a huge thing. On the other hand, it was a small thing locally, in some ways. I haven't even told you about when we had a leafleting we did of Bank of America; one leafleting we had this huge coalition all over the state—I think we were at forty Bank of America branches one day, and then six months later we were at 400, over a third of their branches on the same day, and it was thousands of people that took part in this leafleting, all sorts of people in these eenie-weenie little towns all over. It was on a Friday, and I always said, Bank of America I knew was not golfing that next day, because this stuff just showed up from everywhere. This was in '79. It was great, it was great. It was little towns all over. I finally drove through one, Lincoln, and I always would see it going back and forth to Tahoe, and I finally drove through it when I went to visit my aunt and uncle, right in the middle of the heartland, all these little towns all over, people doing this leafleting. It was really neat.[1]

—Milo Anne Hecathorn, northern California divestment activist

The disintegrating regional and internal framework of apartheid raised U.S. public awareness of southern Africa. The onus of sustaining popular interest lay on the anti-apartheid movement. Organizations had to overcome the barriers constituted by the limited visibility of domestic institutional ties to Africa and traditional aversions to recognizing the racial dimensions of foreign policy. They had to uncover and politicize a matrix of American ties to the production and distribution of wealth and power—and poverty and violence—in South Africa. Two Chicago area activists, Hal Baron of the Campaign for a Democratic Foreign Policy and Prexy Nesbitt of the Amilcar Cabral Collective, developed a 1976 working paper for local groups that had enduring national organizational appeal. They emphasized the need for solid organization from the ground up:

> Since there is no broad movement left over from the anti-Vietnam struggle, a new one will have to be built. It must be built step by step, singling out

specific issues that grow from one another. And it must design programs for the particular constituencies that it hopes to bring together into an eventual broad coalition. Such programs should be formulated to a degree in ways that link international and domestic issues, i.e., to include an aspect that meet needs of the constituency being appealed to. Such formulations stand in contrast to general moral appeals or the passing on of a general scholarly understanding.[2]

Expanding the Movement

Consistent with a political process interpretation, this section examines how sustained interaction with established institutions strengthened the movement's organizational capacity. Traditionally, few if any occasions existed in which citizens could directly engage foreign policy issues. As southern African problems penetrated U.S. domestic politics, activists identified a wider range of targets and mobilization tactics.[3] Picketing, demonstrations, and rallies often attracted media attention, but less visible forms of participation such as seminars, discussion groups, films, and letter writing provided expressive benefits to diverse components of the movement's enlarged constituency. Dennis Chong defines expressive benefits as those that offer participants opportunities to "voice their convictions, affirm their efficacy, share in the excitement of a group effort, and take part in the larger currents of history."[4]

These diverse areas of struggle enabled participants to define targets of opposition while forging alliances and solidarity networks. Unlike domestic issues, apartheid was not amenable to direct observation. The multiplication of sites for contesting apartheid thus gave groups the opportunity to create powerful interpretive linkages between local experience and racial inequality in South Africa. AFSC field organizer Jerry Herman perceived his activist role as focused on

> education, activism and organizing, trying to get people to do something and do it in an organized way and then to hook it back into the bigger movement. From holding meetings, all the great films on South Africa were around, to show stuff, to be local organizers but also to hook into the national thing, we had a United States anti-apartheid newsletter to alert people to what was happening to try to keep the major movement streams in line so people could hook in and to give folks recognition. Because you can't make a movement without recognizing people's attributes.[5]

Transformation of the movement's organizational capacity is closely aligned with responses to openings in three areas. First, the challenge to apartheid benefited from the tolerance that demands for foreign policy reform in the post-Vietnam era created. Second, because established institutions adhered to Cold War zero-sum interpretations of South African–American relations, it became necessary to develop viable investment and policy alternatives, loosen conventional rigidities, and make possible broader coalitions for some movement groups. Third, activists used the resulting moderate climate to construct a putative referendum on human rights and racial discrimination.

Anti-apartheid activism sharpened its political edge by engaging in both assimilative and confrontational activities. Assimilative, or inside, strategies included lobbying, election campaigning, petitioning, and litigation, whereas confrontational, or outside, approaches employed demonstrations, civil disobedience, and other publicity-seeking methods. The dominant strategies employed by various wings of the movement reflected differences in group resources, subcultures, goals, and assessments of efficacy.[6]

In response to the arrival of the first post-Watergate congressional class, the Washington Office on Africa noted "that electing the right person and educating him or her on southern Africa issues may be more effective and easier than converting incumbents who have an established position." WOA realized that South Africa had to be made immediate to Americans. "We need to find ways to better link our support for southern African liberation with the economic and political struggles of Americans at home, in both lobbying, or specific legislation, and in long-term electoral politics."[7] WOA subsequently concentrated on developing southern Africa–orientation sessions for legislators and staffers and diversifying the range of its interactions with congressional committees. Its biennial *Election Notes on Africa* offered evaluations of the candidates' positions on Africa policy issues and a list of questions to assist constituent appraisal of representatives.

The search for relevance led activists to desire a stronger anti-apartheid movement among African Americans and more forthright organizational efforts to identify and exploit a black foreign affairs interest. Sylvia Hill illustrates how this strategy unfolded:

[W]e felt that the role of solidarity groups in the U.S. was not to take an ultraleft position because it wasn't gonna get us anywhere in terms of influencing policy here in the United States; that if you really critique the problems of the struggle of the people of South Africa, for example, their problem was a policy problem in the United States. You know, corporate support, and governmental support of the regime. So, as a solidarity group, our focus had to be on not, you know, kind of talking about getting rid of capitalism there, but to really talk about what has to happen here, in terms of policy, governmental and corporate alliances with the regime there. So we, you know, kind of focused our energies on how do we do that, you know, how do we position ourselves so that we are more mainstream than we are far left. Because having a far left position on this was not going to be useful to move this movement along at this point in history. And therefore, you know, working with congressional people, working with mainstream groups who tend to vote and tend to have mainstream constituencies that vote and tend to write letters and tend to make phone calls in terms of vocalizing their views, we decided that was where we could best make our contribution.[8]

In September 1976, the Congressional Black Caucus invited representatives from groups such as the NAACP, Operation Push, the National Council of Negro Women, and Africare to participate in the Black Leadership Conference on Southern Africa. The conference resolutions called on the United States to support comprehensive UN sanctions against South Africa. The body endorsed armed struggle by liberation movements against the white minority governments of the region.[9] But most important, the conference laid the foundations for TransAfrica, a lobby designed to organize and mobilize the African-American electorate in support of more progressive policies toward Africa.

TransAfrica incorporated in July 1977 and began lobbying Congress in May 1978. It deepened the insider capabilities of apartheid's enemies. Just as the Congressional Black Caucus embodied the gains of the civil rights movement, TransAfrica represented an effort to expand black electoral power beyond established policy boundaries. One of its first campaigns targeted legislators whose districts had black populations of at least 10 percent. Besides alerting legislators to the potentially destabilizing effects of black voting blocs on congressional elections, TransAfrica organized networks of black elected officials, civil rights organizations, church groups, academics, and African diplomats to closely monitor government responses to apartheid. "We lobbied on the Hill," TransAfrica staffer Cecilie Counts recalled.

> We tried to get in touch with influential African Americans who could lobby on the Hill, we kept in touch with governors or mayors, black mayors, black state elected officials, black school board members, black doctors, black lawyers, people who, again, had the capability and understanding to understand the need to write a fairly sophisticated letter, fairly quickly, this is before the fax, before E-mail. People had to actually put things in the mail or have their secretary put it in the mail.[10]

Counts realized the importance of ongoing community contacts. "TransAfrica wouldn't have anything to work with if we didn't have those lists of black school board officials, black mayors, black city council members, black state elected officials," she noted.[11] The fusion of popular electoral activism and elite group sponsorship afforded the organization greater respectability and magnified its capacity to challenge the Democratic Party and the Carter administration.[12] The Washington presence of lobbyists against apartheid constituted informal oversight of official responses to southern Africa racial problems.

Divestment provided the anti-apartheid movement with another major instrument. The basic objective of divestment was to bring pressure to bear on corporate activity in South Africa by encouraging individual and institutional investors such as local governments, universities, and pension funds to sell their shares of stock in corporations connected with the maintenance of apartheid. Divestment could mean total withdrawal, or it could be selective. Investors could be assisted in acquiring alternative socially responsible investments and even encouraged to sign the Sullivan Principles. Divestment activism capitalized on the sense of urgency and represented a new way to use economic sanctions as a weapon of change. It offered practical alternatives to uncritical acceptance of U.S. investment in South Africa's profitable economy. Divestment enabled opponents of apartheid to go beyond expression of moral outrage and furnished practical solutions that transcended specific crisis situations. The scope and breadth of divestment activities offered unlimited coalition and constituency-building opportunities, incorporating confrontational as well as assimilative strategies.

Demands for economic disengagement from South Africa began in the mid-1960s, but effective strategies did not emerge until the rise of shareholder activism a decade later. Shareholder groups failed to achieve corporate withdrawal, but they contributed to the movement's ability to generate and disseminate information. They simultaneously made it more difficult and more necessary for corporate and institutional investors to justify their presence in South Africa.

Preparing requests for corporations to divest required compiling a complex set of data on the performance of a particular company and how its operations fit into the larger structure of South African racial inequality. Divestment advocates engaged in their own research and relied on academic Africanists. They also tapped the data bases of the Investor Responsibility Research Center, which published reports on controversial social and political issues that affect corporate and institutional investor decisionmaking.[13] This fact-finding strengthened shareholder claims and put resources and information in circulation for other groups mounting divestment drives.

As the number of internal actions against corporate engagement increased, responding to them consumed larger shares of management time and energy. According to a study by Thomas N. Gladwin and Ingo Walter on corporate management of political conflicts, the number of human rights proxy resolutions at stockholders' meetings of firms involved in southern Africa increased from 17 in 1976 to 28 in 1977 and to 33 in 1978. The growing "hassle factor" disrupted the routine manner in which businessmen were accustomed to handling South African affairs.[14] Executives of several companies operating in South Africa conceded the significance of the hassle factor in a fall 1980 *Business Week* article. They acknowledged "the blend of South African constraints, polemics back home from anti-apartheid spokesmen, and pressure from stockholding churches, universities, and other institutions on U.S. companies to divest themselves of their S.A. operations."[15] A report presented by financial analyst Joan Bavari at a 1980 Boston conference on public investment in South Africa indicated that companies not involved in South Africa performed better than those that did.[16]

The divestment campaign coincided with lessened criticism of Pretoria from the Carter administration and widening corporate acceptance of the Sullivan Principles. South Africa remained intransigent. In June 1977, ACOA launched the Committee to Oppose Bank Loans to South Africa (COBLSA), an effort coordinated with members of Congress, more than forty national church groups, student and community groups, and labor unions to pressure banks to withhold loans from South Africa until it changed its racial policies. A few months later, the Interfaith Center on Corporate Responsibility beefed up its shareholder resolutions in response to the murder of black South African activist Stephen Biko.

Campaigns initiated by ACOA and ICCR targeted banks that had extended loans to South Africa, such as Bank of America, Citibank, Chase Manhattan, Chemical Bank, First Chicago, Manufacturers Hanover, Morgan Guaranty and Trust, and Wells Fargo. The strategy, based on the premise that American financial involvement in South Africa constituted a form of pro-apartheid political intervention, called for national boycotts of the banks. Individual and group depositors were urged to withdraw their assets.

ACOA sponsored a series of conferences from 1979 to 1983 titled "Public Investment in South Africa." Participants developed strategies to increase public awareness of apartheid, make mobilization skills available to greater audiences, and improve coordination.[17] Organizers invited state and local legislators, investment experts, and a wide range of activists to attend. The meetings offered workshops on South African–American relations, the role of banks and corporations, analyses of the Sullivan Principles, and seminars on organizing legislative alternatives to investing in South Africa.

Divestment activity flourished on college campuses, not only in response to rising public concern about apartheid but also as a result of three changes set in motion by civil rights and antiwar–era protests. First, international, area, and ethnic studies had become fixtures in the curriculum, serving as conduits for linking academic and political interest in southern African issues. Second, increased enrollments of African-American and African students broadened the potential base of participants, forums, and organizations. Third, the simultaneous ending of the Vietnam War and escalation of southern Africa conflicts reopened questions about the role of academic institutions in democratic society,[18] specifically about how colleges and universities could be held accountable for profiting from systems of brutal inequality.

The post-Soweto surge of American campus protests began as small groups of vocal activists challenged the administrators and trustees of well-endowed private institutions to examine their portfolios. Student groups contended that divestment would shine the public spotlight on cooperation with Pretoria, thereby prompting further withdrawals and forcing the collapse of the apartheid system. Student protests in spring

May Day march, Boston, 1977. This was part of the wave of actions focusing on connections between U.S. bank loans and state repression in South Africa.

SOURCE: *Southern Africa*, 1977.

1977 produced nearly 1,000 arrests, but campus groups relied less on confrontational actions than on assimilative tactics such as boycotts, teach-ins, and public forums with university officials. Over the next two years, divestment drives led to nearly twenty institutions selectively disposing of holdings with companies involved in South Africa. The ICCR estimated that between 1976 and 1983, calls for divestment led to disposal of approximately $150 million worth of institutionally owned stock.[19]

The momentum and rapid institutional responses generated by campus divestment drives in the late 1970s suggested an unlimited potential for this strategy. Closer examination of both organizational and situational factors reveals both its achievements and limitations. Protest activity concentrated in three regions of the country: private institutions in the

Demonstrators protesting NBC's 1979 telecasting of a boxing match held in Pretoria, South Africa.

SOURCE: *Southern Africa*, 1979.

Northeast, a combination of large state universities and private liberal arts colleges in the Midwest, and scattered public institutions in northern California, Oregon, and Washington. Counts illustrates the array of proximate activities in the Washington, D.C.–New York corridor:

> I think the direct response to Soweto was protest marches—that's all I concretely remember. I mean, this was the '70s, my brain is a little fuzzy. It seemed like one big long protest march. But I just remember there was an upsurge of organizing. Soweto actually happened. I for example, was in between college years, like a lifeguard, working, so I would come off work and join a candlelight vigil or something like that. When I was in New Jersey, in between those college years, I was close enough to New York City that I could hop over to the village or whatever to participate in whatever big was going on. When I was in D.C. there was the—"June 16th," I think we called it—there was a coalition that evolved out of Soweto here. So I came back to D.C. and then was part of the Howard community and there were things at the White House, protests, picket lines, candlelight vigils—it all starts to blur together.[20]

Much of the coordination for the campus drive came from a group of Stanford University students who established the South Africa Catalyst Project in 1977 to provide information on U.S. business activities in South Africa and develop more effective organizational skills on campus.[21] The project produced a monthly newsletter, distributed handbooks on how to set up campus protests, and assisted in coordinating the nationwide "Week of Action Against Apartheid," in April 1979.

Although pursuit of divestment added clout to campus anti-apartheid struggles, it also apprised activists of several enduring obstacles facing the movement. For the most part, campus activity seldom went beyond private institutions and flagship state universities in the regions identified above. Besides extending the geographic reach and social-class range of their constituencies, campus activists faced the challenges of offsetting the loss of students who had completed the four-year academic cycle that began in fall 1975 with protests over covert involvement in Angola's civil war.[22] They also had to dissuade campus decisionmakers from embracing the "moderate" Sullivan Principles instead of more comprehensive divestment. San Francisco Bay Area labor activist Leo Robinson remembered the unreliability of university student group contributions.

> I went to a few meetings up there, but I understood then as I understand now that the students can only go so far and they do their thing within that circle and then when the summer vacation comes they disappear or when they graduate. It's not a long-term thing, it's a good thing and you support

them when you can, any way you can, but you understand that they are not prime movers in anything. They do things with students, but students, they have an effect and they have a visibility but in the main they don't . . . their activities are confined to campus, let me put it to you like that.[23]

These difficulties converged with rising conservatism in the Carter administration and the electorate, prompting several strategy conferences that reassessed the direction of the campus movement. Joshua Nessen, coordinator of the ACOA campus project, asserted that divestment drives had energized the student left and deflated corporate pretensions. Campus activists nevertheless needed better communication with antinuclear and antiracist movements, Nessen contended, so that these constituencies could mutually support rather than detract from one another.[24]

Subsequent conferences elaborated on this desire to attach antiapartheid activism to broader peace and justice agendas. In the fall of 1979, students at twelve historically black colleges met at Morgan State University with Zimbabwean and South African representatives of the liberation movements to forge alliances between anti-apartheid activism and struggles in African-American communities. A Columbia University organizing conference similarly concluded that the single-issue strategy had limited utility and emphasized the need to link movements for racial injustice in southern Africa to both Central American struggles and local concerns. Shortly thereafter, student groups developed plans for an annual fortnight of coordinated anti-apartheid activities from March 21, the date of the Sharpeville massacre, until April 4, the anniversary of Martin Luther King Jr.'s assassination.[25]

The linkage of anti-apartheid with domestic concerns captured the interest and imagination of community-based groups operating in cities and counties nationwide. Activists in Berkeley and Davis, towns in California with strong university movements, furnished much of the impetus for using local government as a site for launching anti-apartheid programs. Groups sponsored measures for city council and voter approval that withdrew municipal funds from banks lending money to South Africa. The funds would be redeposited in banks that had severed their ties to the regime or in those that invested in domestic development projects. Cities also formed community task forces to explore additional ways to break the bonds with apartheid.[26]

California led the way in mobilizing pension funds as anti-apartheid weapons. The state, chiefly through the agency of Governor Edmund Brown Jr.'s Office of Planning and Research, began exploring the feasibility of using its nearly $20 billion in retirement holdings[27] to influence corporations with South African ties. By the early 1980s, the governor's of-

Massachusetts activists at state legislative hearings on divestment in 1983. Massachusetts was the site of the first successful statewide divestment drive.

SOURCE: *Southern Africa,* 1983.

fice had established a public investment task force and offered resources to groups that wanted the state to disengage from apartheid. This included information about the state's assets, schedules of meetings, procedures for introducing motions, and ways to open meetings to the public. This facilitated student action on divesting University of California endowment and retirement funds. In 1982, the boards of directors of the California Teachers' Retirement System pension fund and the California Public Employees' Retirement System voted to divest from companies with connections to South Africa.

Similar initiatives in Minnesota, Michigan, and Connecticut underlined the threat to withdraw nearly $200 billion of invested public-employee pension funds and other public funds from firms conducting business in South Africa. Gary, Indiana, and Washington, D.C., cities with both electoral and demographic black majorities, voted to divest in 1983. These municipalities not only extended the reach of divestment but also employed other tactics such as selling the stock of companies that provided strategic products to South African security forces and seeking alternative investments. As these actions spread from city to city and from state to state, they caught the attention of the business community. The IRRC's David Hauck believed that "it is something that makes the companies sit up and take notice. It could represent a direct loss of sales. Divesting a stock is symbolic, but when New York City refuses a bid, that's money out of your pocket."[28]

Church and campus-based activism had acquired higher levels of visibility in the anti-apartheid movement. Labor unions could also exert multiple pressures on the system. Jeremy Rifkin and Randy Barber, in their book *The North Shall Rise Again: Pensions, Politics, and Power in the 1980s*, estimated that union pension funds, which were growing at more than 10 percent per year, totaled more than $500 billion nationwide.[29]

The International Longshoremen and Warehousemen Union, especially its San Francisco Bay Area chapters, showed the way in asserting the rights of members to influence investment decisions. Following the independence of Angola and Mozambique in 1974, Bay Area longshoremen formed the Southern African Liberation Committee and mounted a steady campaign of education, coalition building, and anti-apartheid action. Union struggles over apartheid proved fertile grounds for developing alliances between blacks and whites, between campus and community, and were also instrumental in widening the stateside contacts of African liberation movement representatives.[30]

The divestment issue had exposed the limitations of a single-issue strategy, making it clear that the cause of racial justice in South Africa benefited from linkage with the human rights movement generally. The

National Black United Front youth supporters at 1980 Soweto Day rally in New York. By incorporating youth into the struggle, this surge of U.S. activism selectively borrowed from Soweto and the 1960s civil rights movement.

SOURCE: *Southern Africa*, 1982.

Southern Africa Project of the Lawyers' Committee for Civil Rights addressed this issue in trying to ensure that federal courts recognized international law. Formed in 1967, the Southern Africa Project in its early years concentrated most of its resources on assisting South African attorneys defend opponents of apartheid. In the 1970s, the project initiated a series of domestic proceedings to strengthen compliance in the national legal system with antiracist measures derived from UN policies. Project lawyers confronted the *New York Times* in 1974 for including South African jobs with racially discriminatory criteria in its classified section. In another case, it appealed to the Civil Aeronautics Board to deny South African Airways new route permits.[31] Both cases failed, but they exposed the manner in which business conduct quietly and routinely underwrote racial oppression. Also, the fear of further international scrutiny forced South African authorities to abandon some of their most egregious

Picketers at 1978 U.S.–South Africa Davis Cup matches at Vanderbilt University, Nashville, Tennessee.

SOURCE: *Southern Africa*, 1978.

segregationist practices such as listing race as a condition of employment and segregated seating of airline passengers.

Cultural programs flourished in response to South Africa's employment of sports and culture to project more favorable images in the aftermath of international media coverage of state violence. The earliest use of cultural events to spread awareness about apartheid dates to the late 1960s. when black South African exiles such as Hugh Masekela, Miriam Makeba, and Ibrahim Abdullah informed as well as entertained their audiences through music. Later, the works of playwright Athol Fugard (*Sizwe Bansi Is Dead,* and *Master Harold and the Boys*) drew critical acclaim and became fixtures on campuses and conventional theater circuits.[32]

Protests against the fall 1981 U.S. tour by a South African rugby team, the Springboks. A range of sporting events—boxing, tennis, and rugby—emerged as major sites for anti-apartheid groups to mobilize opposition to U.S. collaboration with South Africa.

SOURCE: *Southern Africa,* 1981.

These venues enabled black South Africans to speak directly to Americans about apartheid, rather than having their experiences interpreted.

Sports and film provided additional channels for anti-apartheid sentiments. In 1978, the Coalition for Human Rights, which consisted of the ACOA, the NAACP, and the National Urban League, protested the presence of a South African team at the Davis Cup tennis matches at Vanderbilt University. Veteran anti-apartheid activist Richard Lapchick organized demonstrations against a South African rugby team, the Springboks, at games in New York state during fall 1981.[33] Documentary films became movement resources in 1976, when a small San Francisco film distributor called California Newsreel (which later became the Southern Africa Media Center) began carrying an extensive list of critical films on South Africa such as *Last Grave at Dimbaza, You Have Struck a Rock,* and *South Africa Belongs to Us.* Activists organized boycotts and demonstrations against distribution of South African state propaganda films such as *The Wild Geese,* and *Games for Vultures.*[34]

Protesters at a 1978 New York performance of Ipi-Tombi, a South African government-sponsored play. These campaigns contested efforts by South Africa to camouflage broadening of its programs of separate development.

SOURCE: *Southern Africa, 1983.*

The momentum of the cultural wing continued through the mid-1980s when it confronted South African government efforts to lure American athletes and entertainers to perform there. Booking agents working on behalf of the Republic often targeted African American performers, whose presence seemingly offered a degree of legitimacy to the state's cosmetic reforms. Groups such as the Patrice Lumumba Coalition, African Jazz Artist Society and Studies (AJASS), and the United Nations Centre Against Apartheid in New York City successfully countered this ploy by organizing domestic boycotts of artists who yielded to Pretoria's blandishments.

The publicity associated with big-name entertainers helped rouse black community involvement in the anti-apartheid movement. When guaranteed big paychecks enticed popular recording artists such as Ray Charles, the O'Jays, the Temptations, Roberta Flack and Stephanie Mills to agree to perform in South Africa, boycott activists created the Coalition to End Cultural Collaboration with South Africa (Table 6.1). Coalition leaders realized that the failure to fully exploit the cultural arm had restricted access to potentially significant constituencies. "We think this can be a very good organizing tool," Elombe Brath, cochair of the Patrice Lumumba Coalition contended, "a process of raising people's consciousness about the situation in South Africa—to try to inform these musicians and the general public. We think this is very important, particularly in the case of youth, and most particularly in the case of Black youth, who often don't have a consciousness around South Africa. They worship these stars, know all about them, how much money they make, how many clothes they have, everything. When they come to a concert they see their particular star is being boycotted. About what? About South Africa? What's so wrong about South Africa? And they start to see."[35]

On the surface, the sheer magnitude of the entertainment industry made the tasks confronting the coalition overwhelming. Through a combination of assimilative and confrontational strategies, however, the coalition effectively derailed efforts to marshal talent in the service of apartheid. The coalition created an artists' relations committee that worked with musicians, record companies, and radio broadcasters to inform them about apartheid and the role that African-American performers were to play in it. Artists such as Roberta Flack, Phyllis Hyman, Gladys Knight and Third World canceled previously scheduled engagements, while the O'Jays ended their brief tour early and agreed to sponsor a conference encouraging others to join the boycott.

African-American artists Ray Charles, Stephanie Mills, and Millie Jackson resisted coalition appeals and honored their contractual obligations to South Africa, thus becoming boycott targets. Boycotts focused on club rather than concert hall performances because the former depended on

TABLE 6.1   Entertainers Boycotted in 1982 for Performing in South Africa

America	Chick Corea	"Dr. Johnny Fever"	Stephanie Mills	The Staple Singers
Bob Anderson	Andrew Crouch	Jimmy Bo Horne	Liza Minelli	Edwin Star
Paul Anka	Henry "Manolito"	Susan Howard	Monk Montgomery	Candi Staton
David Baca	Darrow	Janis Ian	James Moody	Dakota Staton
Josephine Baker	Joe Dolan	David Jackson	Olivia Newton-John	The Supremes
Cliff Barnes	Lou Donaldson	Millie Jackson	Linda Oliphant	Brian Tarff
Shirley Bassey	Lamont Dozier	Willis "Gator Tail"	The Osmonds	The Temptations
George Benson	The Drifters	Jackson	Charles Pace	Rufus Thomas
Brook Benton	Jack duPree	Jack Jones	Wilson Pickett	Timmy Thomas
C. L. Blast	Ecstasy Passion &	Tom Jones	The Platters	Bross Townsend
Ernest Borgnine	Pain	Fern Kinney	Barbara Ray	Tina Turner
Beach Boys	Carla Fontana	Eartha Kitt	Helen Reddy	Stanley Turrentine
Gwen Brisco	George Forest	Louis Lane	Della Reese	Two Tons of Fun
Shirley Brown	Midel Fox	Jaime Laredo	Tim Reid "Venus	The Variations
Nina Burrell	Buddy de Franco	Mary Larkin	Flytrap"	Village People
Glen Campbell	Aretha Franklin	Jerry Loren	Richard Roundtree	Lovelace Watkins
Colin Carr	Gloria Gaynor	Main Ingredient	Telly Savalas	Al Wilson
Clarence Carter	Terry Gibbs	Peter Mancer Dancers	Leo Sayer	Jimmy Witherspoon
Monk Channing	Nikki Giovanni	& Reborn	Shirley Scott	Betty Wright
Ray Charles	Francis Grier	Ann Margaret	George Shearing	Robert Wright
Cher	Richard Hatch	Johnny Mathis	Sha Na Na	The Younghearts
Jimmy Cliff	Goldie Hawn	Mattison Brothers	Frank Sinatra	Efrem Zimbalist Jr.
Billy Cobham	Isaac Hayes	Curtis Mayfield	Percy Sledge	
Pete & Conte Condoli	Joe Henderson	George McCrae	Jimmy Smith	
Rita Coolidge	Howard Hesseman	Mighty Clouds of Joy	Diane Solomon	

SOURCE: *Southern Africa* (December 1982).

Elombe Brath, cultural boycott activist, leading a demonstration at a Ray Charles concert in New York. Protests against popular entertainers served the dual function of censuring American artists who performed in South Africa and providing opportunities for expanding public awareness about apartheid.

SOURCE: *Southern Africa,* 1983.

selling food and drinks to patrons after the purchase of tickets, whereas the latter used advance sales. Because club operators arranged performance schedules through regional and national circuits, the coalition could identify and target specific venues as well as performers.[36]

Tourism formed another arm of the cultural wing of the anti-apartheid movement. Travel figured prominently in Pretoria's desire to achieve international respectability. Activists targeted the airlines, hotels, and travel agencies involved in these ventures. As the figures in Table 6.2 indicate, tourism declined immediately after the Soweto rebellion but rebounded strongly into the mid-1980s.

The declining importance of anti-apartheid in both the White House and Congress during the Reagan years led the focus of movement activity to shift to the state and local levels. Changes in venue presented activists with an array of issues—control of pension funds, public influence

TABLE 6.2   U.S. Tourist Visits to South Africa, 1976–1983

Year	Number
1976	44,090
1977	38,343
1978	41,521
1979	43,588
1980	48,725
1981	56,828
1982	50,688
1983	57,391

SOURCE: *Yearbook on South Africa* (Johannesburg: South Africa Foundation, 1972–1986).

on how tax dollars are spent, local banking policies, entertainment—that drove deeply into the fabric of daily life. Each issue mobilized a network of groups and produced an action trajectory and a recursive set of opportunities for contacts with policymaking institutions. This made it more likely that the hidden web of domestic connections to apartheid would gain public exposure and retain policy relevance beyond crisis events.

Consciousness-Raising

Evidence suggests that an improved political opportunity structure in the mid-1970s gave anti-apartheid activists increased confidence about the prospects for movement advancement, prompted a pronounced tilt by other groups and institutions toward the movement, and encouraged broader, deeper public questioning of policy toward South Africa. The convergence of the 1976 presidential campaign with intensifying political unrest in South Africa, Rhodesia, and Angola furnished anti-apartheid activists with more access to the executive and legislative branches of federal government than they had ever enjoyed and gave them the momentum to accelerate the disengagement drive. ACOA director George Houser exhibited an early confidence about movement prospects in suggesting that "U.S. policy is no longer dominated by one person. Carter, Young, Mondale and Vance have all made major policy statements on South Africa," Houser asserted. "There has been a replacement of old-line African hands with more liberal experts. South Africa is the key in any effort to refocus policy in the region."[37]

In March 1977, Congress repealed the Byrd Amendment, which reimposed adherence to the UN ban on importation of Rhodesian chrome.

Campus divestment efforts led to at least twenty colleges and universities removing portions of their assets from banks and financial institutions connected to the apartheid system.

Media attention supplied the American public with more information on southern Africa. In 1975, the three television network news programs broadcast a total of seven reports on southern Africa, chiefly airing congressional debate on the Ford administration's request for funds to intervene in the Angolan civil war. As Figure 6.1 indicates, the Soweto uprising, continued regional political instability, and military activity substantially increased media coverage. The attention that mainstream

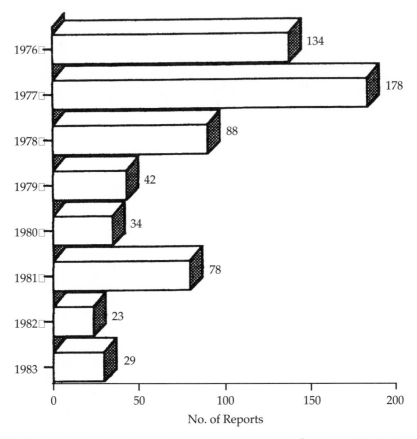

FIGURE 6.1   Television Network News Coverage of South Africa, 1976–1983 (number of reports)

SOURCE: *Television News Index and Abstracts* (Nashville, Tenn.: Vanderbilt Television News Archives, 1976–1983).

TABLE 6.3   U.S. Opinion of Apartheid, 1977 and 1981

	1977 (% responding)	*1981 (% responding)*
Apartheid is justified	12	11
Apartheid is not justified	63	74
Not sure	26	15

SOURCE: Harris Survey, release no. 86 (October 1981).

journalists paid to southern Africa was a coup for anti-apartheid groups because it allowed them to divert their energies and modest resources to fund-raising and strategy development and enhanced their legitimacy in the eyes of policymakers.

Changes in public perceptions of South Africa during the years 1977–1981 suggest that the issues raised by anti-apartheid activists had gained support among significant segments of American society. A Harris poll conducted in 1977, and again in 1981, illustrates the change. A 1979 Public Agenda Foundation study similarly demonstrates that although a majority of respondents feared that South Africa could become another Vietnam, they endorsed the use of some form of government intervention to ensure respect for basic human rights.[38] As shifting public attitudes revealed less tolerance for apartheid and respondents could identify policy options other than adherence to Pretoria, movement organizations became more aggressive and imaginative in eliciting official responses to an increasingly salient issue (Table 6.3).

Conclusion

The period from 1976–1983 represented a watershed in the development of anti-apartheid activism. A chain of actionable issues—the civil war in Rhodesia-Zimbabwe, the Soweto uprisings, the murder of black activist Steve Biko by South African police, and the Sullivan Principles, a controversial ethical code for American corporations in South African—forced Washington officials to qualify their support for official South African policy and the politics of other white-settler regions in the region. Jimmy Carter, elected president with substantial black support, appeared to grant activists access to an administration committed to elevating the policy priority of Africa and human rights.

The momentum established from 1976 to 1978 evaporated, however, when Carter retreated on earlier rhetoric and vital allies in the executive and legislative branches left office. State- and local-level struggles continued to produce important victories. Divestment activities expanded and anti-apartheid organizations effectively joined with peace, human rights, and black electoral activist groups. Even Ronald Reagan's election in 1980, which reduced access to foreign policy decisionmakers, nevertheless contributed to the growth of actionable issues. Constructive engagement temporarily enabled Pretoria to maintain its militarism at home and in the region and to cultivate public support through its consulates and tourism. South African audacity and Reagan's decision to provide covert support to antigovernment UNITA rebels in Angola refocused attention on the administration as an accomplice in southern African instability.[39] Reagan's policies provided his critics with a list of grievances that highlighted the connections between racial inequality at home and abroad.

Anti-apartheid activists built a network of national and local groups to encourage policymakers to reassess institutional connections to apartheid. Divestment formed the backbone of these activities, and divestment campaigns enabled movement organizations to withstand the stresses of the Reagan policy shift. Organizations mobilized the public by emphasizing U.S. institutional commitments to maintaining racial inequality in South Africa and pointing out the availability of effective alternatives.

The most dramatic changes emerged from the political environment. The foreign policy process, especially as it involves Africa, is normally restrictive, as dominant interests and institutions such as transnational corporations and the National Security Council successfully block challengers. Political instability in southern Africa afforded anti-apartheid activists in the United States a chance to question the efficacy of Cold War interventionist strategies.[40] Campus and community divestment drives actualized the demand for sanctions in novel ways. Civil rights groups sustained higher levels of black community involvement, and the cultural boycott effectively monitored South African attempts to sanitize its image. These changes provided the movement with more mobilization space and more opportunities to generate wider public support and cultivate international alliances.

Notes

1. Milo Anne Hecathorn, interview by Connie Field, Clarity Film Productions, Berkeley, 1995, p. 39.

2. Hal Baron, Chicago Chapter, Campaign for a Democratic Foreign Policy, and Prexy Nesbitt, Amilcar Cabral Collective, Chicago, "Working Paper for an Alternative to Kissinger's Southern Africa Policy," p. 2. Paper on file at the Washington Office on Africa (hereafter cited as WOA Papers).

3. Janice Love, *The U.S. Anti-Apartheid Movement: Local Activism in Global Politics* (New York: Praeger, 1985), pp. 15–18.

4. Dennis Chong, *Collective Action and the Civil Rights Movement* (Chicago: University of Chicago Press, 1991), p. 74.

5. Jerry Herman, interview by Billy Nessen, Clarity Film Productions, Berkeley, 1996, p. 14.

6. Thomas R. Rochon, "The West European Peace Movement and New Social Movement Theory," in Russell J. Dalton and Manfred Kuechler, eds., *Challenging the Political Order: New Social and Political Movements in Western Democracies* (New York: Oxford University Press, 1990), pp. 108–112.

7. Washington Office on Africa, *Washington Notes on Africa* (October 1975):3–4.

8. Sylvia Hill, interview by Connie Field, Clarity Film Productions, Berkeley, 1996, p. 9.

9. "African American Manifesto on Southern Africa," *Black Scholar* 8, 2 (January–February 1977):27–32.

10. Cecilie Counts, interview by Connie Field, Clarity Film Productions, Berkeley, 1996, p. 9.

11. Ibid., p. 14.

12. Henry F. Jackson, *From the Congo to Soweto: U.S. Foreign Policy Toward Africa Since 1960* (New York: William Morrow, 1982), pp. 123–125.

13. Desaix Myers III, with Kenneth Propp, David Hauck, and David M. Liff, *U.S. Business in South Africa: The Economic, Political, and Moral Issues* (Bloomington: Indiana University Press, 1980).

14. Thomas N. Gladwin and Ingo Walter, *Multinationals Under Fire: Lessons in the Management of Conflict* (New York: John Wiley and Sons, 1985), pp. 158–160; Philip V. White, "The Black American Constituency for Southern Africa, 1940–1980," in Alfred Hero and John Barratt, eds., *The American People and South Africa: Publics, Elites, and Policymaking Processes* (Lexington, Mass.: Lexington Books, 1981), p. 91.

15. "South Africa's Foot-Dragging Vexes U.S. Companies," *Business Week* 2659 (October 20, 1980):56–58.

16. Jennifer Davis, James Cason, and Gail Hovey, "Economic Disengagement and South Africa: The Effectiveness and Feasibility of Implementing Sanctions and Divestment," *Law and Policy in International Business* 15 (1983):562.

17. American Committee on Africa, *Action News* 10 (Fall 1981):1.

18. The number of African students in the United States increased from just over 18,000 in 1975 to more than 43,000 in 1983. U.S. Department of Commerce, Bureau of the Census, *Statistical Abstract of the United States*, 1974–1986; Lawrence F. Stevens and James G. Lubetkin, "American Universities and South Africa," in Hero and Barratt, *The American People and South Africa*, pp. 123–137.

19. Hero and Barratt, *The American People and South Africa*, pp. 127–129; Jonathan Leape, Bo Baskin, and Stefan Underhill, *Business in the Shadow of Apartheid: U.S. Firms in South Africa* (Lexington, Mass.: Lexington Books, 1985), appendix D, pp. 215–216.

20. Counts, interview, pp. 3–4.

21. Lawrence Litvak, Robert Degrasso, and Kathleen McTigue, *South Africa: Foreign Investment and Apartheid* (Washington, D.C.: Institute for Policy Studies, 1978.

22. American Committee on Africa, *Student Anti-Apartheid Newsletter* (December 1979):1.

23. Leo Robinson, interview by Billy Nessen, Clarity Film Productions, Berkeley, 1996, p. 13.

24. Joshua Nessen, "The U.S. Student Anti-Apartheid Movement," testimony presented to UN Committee Against Apartheid Policies, October 19, 1979, on file at the American Committee on Africa, New York, N.Y.; David Hauck, Meg Voorhes, and Glenn Goldberg, *Two Decades of Debate: The Controversy over U.S. Companies in South Africa* (Washington, D.C.: Investor Responsibility Research Center, 1983), p. 26.

25. Danaher, *In Whose Interest? A Guide to U.S.-South Africa Relations* (Washington, D.C.: Institute for Policy Studies, 1984), pp. 182–220.

26. Myers et al., *U.S. Business in South Africa*, p. 283.

27. Ibid., p. 284. The California Teachers' Retirement System had assets of nearly $5.7 billion, the Public Employees Retirement System held $10.7 billion in assets, and the University of California endowment and retirement fund consisted of $2.2 billion.

28. John M. Kline, *State Government Influence in U.S. International Economic Policy* (Lexington, Mass.: Lexington Books, 1983), pp. 196–199; "City, State Actions Force Companies to Take Notice," *Africa News* 24 (May 20, 1985):19.

29. Jeremy Rifkin and Randy Barber, *The North Shall Rise Again: Pensions, Politics, and Power in the 1980s* (Boston: Beacon Press, 1978), p. 84.

30. Robinson, interview, 1996.

31. David Weissbrodt and Georgina Mahoney, "International Legal Action Against Apartheid," *Law and Inequality* 4 (October 1986):485–508; *Guild Practitioner* 34 (1977):52–64.

32. Raphael Gould, "Review: Sizwe Bansi Is Dead and the Island," *Southern Africa* 8, 3 (March 1975):34.

33. "Anti-Apartheid Groups Take Aim at Davis Cup," *Africa News* 10, 7 (February 20, 1978):5; "Stop the South African Rugby Tour," *Action Alert* (July 31, 1981):1.

34. "Film: South Africa Like It Is," *Southern Africa* 12, 8 (September 1979):18–21; "More Dirty Birds—After "Wild Geese," the "Game of Vultures," *Southern Africa* 12, 1 (January 1979):32.

35. Mike Fleshman, "Building the Cultural Boycott," *Southern Africa* 16, 1 (January–February 1983):4.

36. Ibid., p. 5.

37. George Houser, "Preaching Freedom, Investing in Oppression: U.S. Policy in Southern Africa," *Southern Africa Perspectives* 4 (1977):1.

38. Deborah Durfee Barron and John Immerwahr, "The Public Views South Africa: Pathways Through a Gathering Storm," *Public Opinion* 2 (January–February 1979):54–59.

39. Robert Fatton Jr., "The Reagan Policy Toward South Africa: Ideology and the New Cold War," *African Studies Review* 27, 2 (March 1984):57–82.

40. Martin Staniland, "Africa, the American Intelligentsia, and the Shadow of Vietnam," *Political Science Quarterly* 98, 4 (Winter 1983–1984):600.

7

The Free South Africa Movement and the Zenith of Anti-Apartheid Activism, 1984–1987

A principal tenet of a political process model is that social movements grow in importance when established institutions become vulnerable to challenge. Reductions in power disparity between mainstream institutions and insurgent forces often characterize periods of movement strength. The resulting changes in political opportunity render insurgent actions less risky and potentially more successful. The rate of continued movement development depends on the amount of leverage exercised by challengers. If power disparities return to pre-movement levels, the probability of growth diminishes. If the political leverage exercised by insurgents remains high, the probability that the movement will survive and expand increases.[1]

Anti-apartheid movement activity peaked from 1984 to 1986 and commanded unprecedented levels of public and media attention, generating a consensus among diverse organizations and constituencies that policy toward South Africa needed profound change. This stage of heightened activism coincided with escalating violence in South Africa. The combination put greater pressures on policymakers from the federal to local levels and on churches, colleges and universities, and investment managers. However, movement effectiveness at provoking public involvement and institutional responses ironically set forces in motion that eventually led to movement decline. The interested public ultimately failed to endorse tactics that would go beyond sanctions legislation.[2]

The Structure of Political Opportunity

Just weeks before the 1984 presidential election, the Reagan administration was so confident about the efficacy of its "quiet diplomacy" with

South Africa that the U.S. ambassador to the UN refrained from voting on a Security Council resolution condemning apartheid. Reagan's optimism rested on the premise that neither anti-apartheid activism nor business apprehensions about remaining in South Africa posed credible threats to the Pieter Botha regime. Before the year ended, however, rising internal and international opposition to apartheid redefined the course of South African national development and caused one of Reagan's most important foreign policy defeats.

In the early 1980s, the Botha government had taken comfort in an economy continually revitalized by foreign investment and a U.S. policy of "constructive engagement" that tolerated Pretoria's military aggression against neighboring African states. Botha's confidence camouflaged a complex set of factors that separately presented cause for concern and collectively fueled the domestic uprisings that would dramatically restructure the regime's external relations. Even the reforms initiated in response to global scrutiny following Soweto and the sweeping security force campaigns against dissent yielded unintended consequences. Reforms did not preempt demands for black inclusion. They instead precipitated greater instability and uncertainty and further undermined the state's economic base and political legitimacy.

Black trade unionism revived during the 1973 Durban strikes and became a pivotal force in South African industrial life. The Industrial Relations Act of 1979, a measure designed primarily to confine black activism to the workplace, accorded recognition to black worker organizations. This modest opening led to an explosion in union membership, strike activity, and linkages of worker aims to broader anti-apartheid struggles.

Thirty-nine black trade unions in 1979 claimed a membership of just over 800,000. By 1984, the number of unions exceeded 100, and membership soared to nearly 1.5 million. Labor disruptions similarly increased from 101 in 1979 to 469 in 1984. As strikes frequently elicited police response, the state involuntarily erased the distinction between workplace and anti-apartheid activism. Labor activism experienced another boost in December 1985, when the moderate, workplace-oriented Federation of South African Trade Unions (FOSATU) merged with politicized community unions to become the Congress of South African Trade Unions (COSATU). Labor's rapid politicization enabled COSATU to become an "extraparliamentary" anti-apartheid organization.[3]

State attempts to co-opt black unrest in the cities also backfired. Pretoria passed the Black Local Authorities Act in 1982, transferring some control of black urban populations to government-appointed black officials. This system of indirect rule deflected criticism from Pretoria to its puppets. A year later, constitutional revision established a tricameral parliament, incorporating Indians and Coloureds but excluding Africans.

These changes ignited widespread protests in African, Indian, and Coloured communities. The groundswell of community resistance supplied the impetus for nationwide protests from groups that merged into the United Democratic Front.[4]

Mobilizing around the nonracial slogan "Apartheid Divides, UDF Unites," UDF arose as an umbrella organization with a broad ethnic, regional, and demographic base. It employed strategies ranging from elections and consumer boycotts to rallies and conferences in order to reorient public debate, shifting it from a focus on whether ethnic groups should endorse the state's limited participatory schemes to critiques of those arrangements, which left intact the fundamental inequalities that apartheid imposed. UDF's ascent coincided with black labor's rejuvenated power to exploit South African economic instability. It thus enlarged the political space for opposing apartheid, simultaneously garnering and sustaining international attention.

Violent opposition to state co-optative programs invited comparisons to Sharpeville and Soweto, but no one could have predicted the 1984 escalation of the anti-apartheid struggle that signaled its arrival at a new level of engagement. This stage would last for nearly two years, evolving into a general struggle that undermined the legitimacy of the state and effectively nullified its power in major parts of the country. Deepening rebellions reflected the intense polarization of South African society and the state's declining capacity to maintain order.

Fierce protests broke out in the Vaal townships south of Johannesburg on September 3, 1984, the day the new Constitution went into effect. Local issues such as rent strikes and school suspensions triggered the protests, but the new constitutional provisions provided an overarching target. Unrest spread rapidly across the country, as combined school and consumer boycotts, trade union strikes, and ANC sabotage created a mass uprising of unprecedented scope, duration, and intensity. State security forces responded by opening fire on protesters, occupying schools and black townships, and arresting and detaining thousands of activists. By June 1985, a vicious spiral of conflict involving a profoundly repressive state and a militant popular resistance movement claimed more than 500 lives.

Popular willingness to use violence to contest apartheid became the focus of international media reporting on South Africa. The uprising nevertheless transcended physical retaliation against the state. It also differed qualitatively from the Soweto insurrection of eight years before. The protest actions that accompanied Vaal drove deeply into the social fabric of the black community. Alienated students and youth composed the vanguard, but a network of associations involving parents, unions, and community and civic groups also participated. The political culture of resistance exhibited a talent for transforming state intrusions into instruments for further politicization. Funerals for victims of state violence, for example, became political gatherings that drew additional police and army units, thus setting up the cycle for immediate repetition.

The growth of alternative institutions filled the void left by the state's withdrawal from African civic affairs and indicates that the insurrection had progressed beyond cathartic violence. Civic and youth groups in many townships assumed a range of administrative, judicial, education, and welfare functions. Organizing these activities swelled the number of people accountable and multiplied and diversified the roles they played in the movement.[5] The paragovernmental functions exercised by "the people" were not always successful, but the process furnished practical experience in governance and administration, as well as psychological support for challenging regime legitimacy.

The UDF, labor unions, civic associations, and other groups catalyzed popular insurgency, and the rapidly shifting political terrain abetted the ANC's circuitous return to mainstream politics. In its 1985 New Year's message, the ANC enjoined protesters to "make South Africa ungovernable."[6] When the momentum of the insurrection overwhelmed the capacity of the UDF's loose organizational structure, it began broadening its mass appeal by incorporating ANC ideals and slogans into its literature and public communications. By late spring 1985, the state conceded the loss of control over substantial parts of the country, thus directly acknowledging the power of the ANC's provocation.

The American business community in South Africa seized the time to register its own concerns. U.S. companies had been at the forefront of workplace reforms but traditionally deferred to local firms on political matters. But in March 1985, a delegation from the American Chamber of Commerce in South Africa delivered a reform proposal to Minister of Constitutional Development Chris Huenis. The proposal echoed the growing sentiments of South African business groups and encouraged the state to move toward representation of all adults in the national legislature. A group of eighty American executives placed ads in domestic and South African newspapers in April 1985, calling on Pretoria to end legal racial discrimination, begin political negotiations, grant full citizenship to blacks, and end detentions without charge or trial. In September, this group evolved into the U.S. Corporate Council in South Africa, adding to the business community's reform momentum.[7]

Corporations did not confine their efforts to lobbying. As divestment pressures mounted back home, they adopted more visible social agendas. The number of Sullivan Principles signatories in 1985 grew from 129 to 178.[8] Companies began projects to improve the training of black workers and stimulate African entrepreneurship. IBM announced new grants totaling more than $15 million over five years to support literacy skill improvement in black schools. Other corporate endeavors included Goodyear's $6 million education and housing scheme, Mobil Oil's $20 million teacher-training program, and a $10 million pledge from Coca-Cola to support black housing and education. Within two years of the onset of township resistance, American companies had initiated over one thousand "socially responsible" projects.[9]

On July 21, Botha declared a state of emergency and gave police additional powers. Over the next eight months, police arrested or detained more than 10,000 mostly youthful (under twenty-five years old) protesters. State restraints forced UDF to revise its tactics but failed to limit its reach and intensity. UDF-affiliated groups, helped by a growing cadre of street committees, organized consumer boycotts of white-owned shops. They demanded removal of government troops from townships, new school construction, desegregation of store entrances, termination of evictions and relocation, and creation of nonracial municipal councils.[10]

Prolonged strife and a weakening state catapulted local and national business interests into more prominent political roles. In mid-August 1985, local business associations responded to the boycotts by indicating their willingness to remove employment barriers and to end segregation of black workers and consumers. Business organizations also agreed to lobby the state to open the political system to blacks.

As the state displayed little capacity to restore the political stability necessary for economic growth, six national business associations announced plans to turn up the heat on Pretoria. They would press for full participation for all races in political and economic life; guaranteed full citizenship for all South Africans; abolition of forced removals to homelands; a court system capable of administering nonracial justice; and protection for the right of free trade-union organization.[11] Business leaders encouraged the government to begin talks with black leaders and break the stalemate caused by township violence and the state of emergency. In September, a group of elite businessmen took the unprecedented step of meeting with exiled ANC leaders in Zambia. This meeting demonstrated ANC's strength and foiled Pretoria's effort to exclude it as a player in peace negotiations.

The insurrection introduced new power possibilities in domestic politics and quickened international efforts to disengage from South Africa. In September, the European Economic Union (EEC) banned the sale of computers and oil to the troubled republic and canceled nuclear collaboration projects. The Commonwealth nations, with Britain as the major dissenter, also began to consider adopting sanctions, as did the Nordic countries.

South African state actions seemed to exacerbate defiance rather than contain political upheaval. Rumors had circulated in both foreign and domestic circles that a speech by President Botha, scheduled for August

15, 1985, would propose the political incorporation of blacks and thus end the spiraling violence. But instead of announcing major reforms, Botha warned both domestic and foreign critics that his government had been pushed too far already and that concessions were not imminent. Botha's speech, in which he announced that South Africa had crossed the Rubicon and refused to yield any further, was a major turning point in alienating Western governments. The state's hard-line position reinforced the siege mentality of right-wing parties and constituencies but led more moderate whites to follow business leaders in exploring other remedies for the nation's ills.

Botha suspended the state of emergency in March 1986, but renewed violence led to its reimposition three months later. The second state of emergency resulted from major rifts within the state bureaucracy as well as black unrest. Faced with unyielding resistance and the growing momentum of external sanctions campaigns, state security officials rapidly ascended to dominant policymaking positions. These "securocrats" saw their mission as reestablishing state control.[12]

The second state of emergency represented a shift in Pretoria's strategy as it combined infrastructural improvements in black residential areas with increased detention of political activists, press censorship, and de facto military rule. Refined counterrevolutionary tactics disrupted the insurrection's momentum and curtailed foreign news reporting. By early 1987, resistance appeared to have ended, but the stage had already been prepared for more dramatic restructuring of South Africa's external relations.

The U.S. Response to the South African Crisis

At first glance, rising levels of violence in South Africa presented no significant problems for the Reagan administration, because Reagan's overwhelming reelection victory silenced many of his domestic critics. But over the next eighteen months, the protracted struggle in South Africa exposed dissent within the White House bureaucracy over constructive engagement, revealed tensions in the Republican Party, and narrowed Reagan's public credibility.[13] Friction increased within the Reagan administration as the foreign affairs bureaucracy clashed with the president's inner circle of advisers on how to respond to the South African situation. The ensuing climate of uncertainty enabled Congress and state and local officials to pursue new options in responding to apartheid.

Chester Crocker, assistant secretary of state for African affairs and architect of the quiet diplomatic approach toward Pretoria, insisted that sanctions would strip the United States of the leverage needed to persuade Botha to continue the reform process and would undermine the business sector's vanguard role. Crocker viewed constructive engagement as a delicate operation in which the United States would negotiate removal of Cuban troops from Angola, secure Pretoria's pledge to end military aggression against Angola and neighboring black states, and dislodge Namibia from South African control.

Crocker and Secretary of State George Shultz claimed that the United States, unlike Cuba, was neutral, but other members of the administration such as CIA director William Casey, UN ambassador Jeane Kirkpatrick, secretary of defense Caspar Weinberger, White House staffers Patrick Buchanan and Donald Regan, along with allies in the National Security Council, favored open alignment with South Africa. For this inner circle, anticommunism dictated less concern over the delicacies of diplomacy. They held that support for antigovernment guerrillas in Angola and Mozambique and close military and intelligence ties to Pretoria best served American interests in southern Africa. Members of this group exploited their personal and positional access to Reagan and cultivated conservative Republican legislators such as Senators Jesse Helms (R.–N.C.), Jeremiah Denton (R.–Ala.) and such House members as Robert Dornan (R.–Calif.) and Dan Burton (R.–Ind.). They worked closely with South African representatives and agents in the United States and with the network of domestic right-wing groups such as the Heritage Foundation, the American Security Council, the Conservative Caucus and the Cuban-American National Foundation.[14]

Administrative hard-liners fought to use Angola as a surrogate in their battle against the Soviets. They lobbied vigorously for repeal of the Clark Amendment, which Congress had passed in 1976 to counter the Ford administration's interventionist plans for the Angolan civil war. When this failed, hard-liners turned to right-wing groups and to South Africa and Saudi Arabia to covertly assist antigovernment UNITA rebels. According to Crocker and Shultz, these maneuvers weakened Washington's negotiating hand by sending mixed signals about its intentions in the region, especially as international public opinion aligned against South Africa.[15]

As Reagan cautioned the public to resist the urge to demand punitive measures against South Africa, legislators in the president's own party expressed doubts about the wisdom of that advice. The Conservative Opportunity Society (COS), a group of young Republican House members, viewed opposition to apartheid as a critical issue that could broaden the Republican Party's base and generate a post-Reagan consensus that would ensure GOP dominance in national elections. Thirty-five COS members wrote a letter to Bernardus Fourie, the South African ambassador to the United States, warning him that unless Pretoria took genuine steps toward discarding apartheid, Republican party leaders would endorse the sanctions:

We are looking for an immediate end to the violence in South Africa accompanied by a demonstrated sense of urgency about ending apartheid. If such actions are not forthcoming, we are prepared to recommend that the U.S. government take the following two steps:

1. Curtail new American investment in South Africa unless certain economic and civil rights guarantees for all persons are in place.
2. Organize international diplomatic and economic sanctions against South Africa.[16]

Reagan's fantasy of progress and good South African intentions persisted even when publicly available evidence contradicted that perspective and in spite of the COS initiative assaulting the Great Communicator's image. The president snubbed black South African bishop Desmond Tutu, an advocate of sanctions and winner of the 1984 Nobel Peace Prize, during his fall visit to Washington. And only weeks after the first state of emergency, Reagan declared that his critics were mistaken, claiming that apartheid had already ended: "South Africa has eliminated the segregation that we once had in our own country . . . the type of thing where hotels and restaurants and places of entertainment and so forth were segregated—that has all been eliminated."[17]

When critics asserted that constructive engagement served as endorsement of South Africa's killing of black demonstrators, Reagan responded: "But I think to put it that way—that they were simply killed and that the violence was coming totally from the law and order side ignores the fact that there was rioting going on in behalf of others there." "It is significant," he claimed, "that some of those enforcing the law and using guns were also black policemen." Reagan argued that the turmoil resulted from "blacks fighting against blacks, because there's still a tribal situation involved there in that community."[18] To him, apartheid was merely an inconvenience for blacks who had not yet acquired the skills to enter the modern economy. He did not see it as a politically refined, technologically advanced, internationally reinforced system of racial inequality that constrained African life from cradle to grave.

Reagan expressed confidence in business initiative rather than government intervention as the most effective means for promoting change in South Africa. He explained that corporate embrace of the Sullivan Principles merited support because "Sullivan is a black clergyman." As the sanctions drive intensified internationally, Reagan saw punitive actions against Pretoria as unwarranted and unpopular with Africans: "The truth is that most black tribal leaders there have openly expressed their support of American business investment there, because our American businesses go there and observe practices with regard to employees that are not observed by South African companies."[19]

The confounding messages emanating from the White House opened the door for congressional initiative in responding to rising public sentiment for action against South African intransigence. In early June 1985, a sense of urgency prompted the House to pass a sanctions bill (HR-1460) that would ban new corporate investments, bank loans, the importation of Krugerrands, computer sales to the South African government, and mutual nuclear cooperation. The bill included a provision mandating consideration of additional sanctions within twelve months. In spite of staunch opposition from loyal Reagan supporters like Helms, the Senate passed a weaker version of sanctions legislation (S-995) in July, by a 80 to 12 vote. The Senate bill mandated corporate adherence to the Sullivan Principles and consideration of new sanctions after two years. Later that month, a joint House-Senate conference committee adopted the more limited sanctions bill that included bans on bank loans and importation of Krugerrands, restrictions on sales of computer and nuclear products, required corporate use of the Sullivan Principles, and consideration of additional sanctions in one year.

The sanctions bill was a sharp warning to a president adamantly opposed to any punitive actions against South Africa. Faced with the prospect of a congressional override should he veto the bill, Reagan issued Executive Order 12532, a measure designed to co-opt the legislative process and shift the policy momentum back to the White House. The order included bans on federal loans to the South African state and on the sale of computers to its security agencies, limited restrictions on nuclear cooperation with Pretoria, and a formal investigation into the legality of banning importation of Krugerrands. Unlike the congressional bill, the executive fiat made no reference to when the government would consider additional sanctions. It instead called for the creation of a bipartisan committee to examine policy and make recommendations to the secretary of state.

The administration acted swiftly to head off further congressional intervention in South Africa policy, but three other factors heightened the prospects of legislative interference. First, violence in South Africa held the American public's interest. The three major television networks provided unprecedented coverage of events in the republic. Second, South African authorities matched black rebellion with greater levels of repression and mounted renewed attacks against suspected collaborators in neighboring countries. Pretoria's militarism attracted rather than deflected attention and discredited claims made by sanction opponents about the Botha government's good intentions. Third, policymakers continued sending mixed signals about their objectives. Only days after the Senate approved economic sanctions against South Africa, its repeal of the Clark Amendment paved the way for resumption of military assistance to anticommunist Angolan rebels. After Reagan issued the executive order preempting more punitive congressional sanctions, the State Department appointed an ad hoc working group, headed by ambassador-ranked Douglas Hollady, to focus on improving the public presentation rather than the substance of constructive engagement.[20]

Administrative efforts at image enhancement and neutralization of congressional criticism faltered because Pretoria proved reluctant to meet international expectations in its behavior at home and in the region. The sanctions debate regained momentum in Congress during the summer of 1986. In June, the House passed comprehensive sanctions bill HR-4868, which included a complete trade embargo and divestment of all economic holdings in South Africa. Two months later, the Senate passed S-2701, its own version of the bill, incorporating many of the provisions of the 1985 executive order and prohibiting private bank loans and new investments. A joint House-Senate conference committee submitted S-2701 to the full congress as its report, and the bill subsequently passed as the Comprehensive Anti-Apartheid Act of 1986.

Congress again shifted the public burden of responding to apartheid to the executive branch. As in the previous year, Reagan expected to co-opt the legislative process by vetoing the bill and substituting a milder executive order. The president felt that his policies could be vindicated by taking the case to the American people. In a network televised speech on July 22, Reagan remained firm in his defense of South Africa and characterized the sanctions in the congressional bill as "immoral" and "utterly repugnant." He characterized the ANC as "Soviet-armed guerrillas" engaging in "calculated terror," thus releasing Pretoria from any "obligation to negotiate the future of the country with any organization that proclaims a goal of creating a Communist state and uses terrorist tactics and violence to achieve it."[21] Reagan's remarks, drafted by White House staffer Pat Buchanan, a staunch defender of South Africa, did as little to acquit U.S. policy at a time of condemnation at home and abroad as Botha's Rubicon speech had a year earlier.

Reagan's subsequent veto of the sanctions bill encouraged administration hard-liners and their right-wing constituencies but presented a major dilemma for Republican legislators. Overriding the veto meant deserting the president on a key issue, which could aid Democrats eager to tear down Reagan's image as party leader during midterm elections less than two months away. At the same time, failure to override the veto risked negative public association of the GOP with reactionary Southern Senators such as Helms and Denton, who openly sympathized with Pretoria. Mississippi House member Trent Lott explained why this predicament made other Republican candidates nervous: "It's right before an election, and there are a lot of districts with heavy black populations, and members don't want to take a chance of offending them."[22]

Influential GOP senators such as Majority Leader Bob Dole, Richard Lugar, chair of the Foreign Relations Committee, and Nancy Kassebaum, chair of the Subcommittee on African Affairs, repeatedly warned Reagan of the domestic ramifications of his stance on South Africa. Dole, who anticipated entering the battle to succeed Reagan in 1988, recognized that a critical foreign policy decision had become a referendum on the congressional stance on racial discrimination. "Let's face it," he acknowledged. "There's a lot of politics involved. This has now become a domestic civil rights issue."[23]

The president remained unwilling to recognize the strategic significance of the issue for his party. At the height of the sanctions debate, it became apparent that the administration wanted to replace Ambassador Herman Nickel, who had completed his rotation abroad, with a black ambassador, hoping to deflect some of the criticism of constructive engagement. The first candidate, North Carolina businessman Robert J. Brown, withdrew his name when revelations about a scandal surfaced, and a second candidate, Terence A. Todman, then ambassador to Denmark, would not accept the nomination because he believed that U.S. policy toward South Africa lacked credibility.[24]

Reagan then nominated Edward J. Perkins, ambassador to Liberia. Perkins eventually received Senate approval, but the search proved embarrassing for an already embattled administration. Reagan could not be dissuaded from taking these offensive symbolic steps. Although his staff had expended little energy influencing Congress on the vote to override, in a last-ditch effort, the president sent Alan C. Keyes, assistant secretary of state for international organizations, to Capitol Hill to lobby undecided legislators.

With Reagan clearly out of touch with the realities of apartheid and the concerns of the public, members of Congress could justify their vote to override as a necessary intervention in the policy process. In late September, the House voted 317 to 83 in favor of overriding the president's veto, and just days later, the Senate followed suit by a 78 to 21 margin. The bill's major provisions included: (1) prohibition of the importation of South African coal, steel, textiles, uranium, agricultural products, and products produced by South African parastatals, (2) application of these sanctions to South African–controlled Namibia, (3) removal of landing rights of South African airlines in the United States and of U.S. airlines in South Africa, (4) a ban on deduction of South African taxes from U.S. corporate income, (5) prohibition of new corporate investments in South

Africa, and (6) interdiction on deposits in American banks by South African governmental agencies. Passage of the Anti-Apartheid Act coincided with sanctions packages legislated in Great Britain and the Commonwealth states, the EEC, and Japan.[25]

Conclusion

U.S. policy toward South Africa during most of Reagan's second term exposed weaknesses in the traditional Cold War approach toward apartheid and helped create new opportunities for anti-apartheid activism. White House intransigence impugned the credibility of national security and foreign policy experts, created skepticism about presidential judgment, and placed apartheid on the docket as a domestic racial issue. By energizing constituencies predisposed toward extending civil rights principles abroad, opposition to apartheid acquired an honorary exemption from the Cold War categorical treatment of African policy concerns. The domestic ramifications of apartheid temporarily granted it the status of a moral issue; or, more cynically, blacks became in this instance honorary whites. Critics of administration policy also benefited from the strategic positions occupied by Congressional Black Caucus members. Apartheid had always been one of the CBC's major policy concerns, and by 1985, many CBC members had gained seniority and leadership positions on powerful committees. They showed a readiness to use that leverage against a president viewed as hostile to the interests of African Americans.[26]

Notes

1. Doug McAdam, *Political Process and the Development of Black Insurgency, 1930–1970* (Chicago: University of Chicago Press, 1982), p. 146.

2. Danny Schecter, "South Africa: Where Did the Story Go? *Africa Report* 33, 2 (1988):27; Pauline H. Baker, *The United States and South Africa: The Reagan Years* (Washington, D.C.: Council on Foreign Relations, 1989); John Lofland, "Consensus Movements: City Twinning and Derailed Dissent in the American Eighties," *Research in Social Movements, Conflict, and Change* 11:163–196.

3. Robert M. Price, *The Apartheid State in Crisis: Political Transformation in South Africa, 1975–1990* (New York: Oxford University Press, 1991), pp. 162–164; William H. Kaempfer, James A. Lehman, and Anton D. Lowenberg, "Divestment, Investment Sanctions, and Disinvestment: An Evaluation of Anti-Apartheid Policy Instruments," *International Organization* 41, 3 (Summer 1987):473.

4. Tom Lodge and Bill Nasson, *All Here, and Now: Black Politics in South Africa in the 1980s* (New York: Ford Foundation and the Foreign Policy Association, 1991), pp. 58–62.

5. Ibid., pp. 135–139.

6. Ibid., p. 76.

7. Ibid., p. 17.

8. Richard W. Hull, *American Enterprise in South Africa* (New York: New York University Press, 1990), p. 334.

9. Ibid., p. 335.

10. Lodge and Nasson, *All Here, and Now*, pp. 78–79.

11. David Hauck, *Can Pretoria Be Moved? The Emergence of Business Activism in South Africa* (Washington, D.C.: Investor Responsibility Research Center, 1986), p. 14.

12. Lodge, and Nasson, *All Here, and Now*, pp. 89–90.

13. Wilbur Edel, *The Reagan Presidency: An Actor's Finest Performance* (New York: Hippocrene Books, 1992), pp. 179–183.

14. James M. Scott, *Deciding to Intervene: The Reagan Doctrine and American Foreign Policy* (Durham, N.C.: Duke University Press, 1996), pp. 124–126.

15. Ibid., pp. 120–121; Chester Crocker, *High Noon in Southern Africa: Making Peace in a Rough Neighborhood* (New York: W. W. Norton, 1992), pp. 292–297; George Shultz, *Turmoil and Triumph: My Years as Secretary of State* (New York: Charles Scribner's Sons, 1993).

16. Congressional letter to South African Ambassador, December 4, 1984, in Baker, *The United States and South Africa*, appendix B.

17. U.S. President, *Public Papers of the Presidents of the United States, Ronald Reagan* (1984), p. 1873; Alan Cowell, "Bishops Criticize Pretoria's Police," *New York Times*, December 7, 1984; Mark Green and Gail MacColl, *Reagan's Reign of Error: The Instant Nostalgia Edition* (New York: Pantheon, 1987), pp. 144–149; *Weekly Compilation of Presidential Documents*, 21, 35 (September 3, 1985):1004.

18. "President's News Conference on Foreign and Domestic Issues," *New York Times*, March 22, 1985; U.S. President, *Public Papers of the Presidents of the United States, Ronald Reagan* (1986), p. 801.

19. U.S. President, *Public Papers of the Presidents of the United States, Ronald Reagan* (1986), p. 666; U.S. President, *Public Papers of the Presidents of the United States, Ronald Reagan* (1984), p. 1881.

20. Baker, *The United States and South Africa*, p. 41.

21. "Ending Apartheid in South Africa," address by President Ronald Reagan, July 22, 1986, in Baker, *The United States and South Africa*, appendix C.

22. "Hill Overrides Veto of South Africa Sanctions," *Congressional Quarterly Weekly Report* 44, 40 (October 4, 1986):2339.

23. Pauline H. Baker, "The Sanctions Vote: A GOP Milestone," *New York Times*, August 26, 1986.

24. "Reagan and the Limits of Leverage," *Africa Report* 31, 5 (September–October 1986):12–15.

25. For a description of the bill, see Senate Bill 2701, Calendar no. 775, 99th Cong., 2d sess.; "Sanctions Levied Against South Africa . . . by Nation and Economic Communities," *Congressional Quarterly Almanac* 42 (1986):368–369.

26. William J. Foltz, "United States Policy Toward South Africa: Is One Possible?" in Gerald J. Bender, James S. Coleman, and Richard L. Sklar, eds., *African Crisis Areas and U.S. Foreign Policy* (Berkeley and Los Angeles: University of California Press, 1986), pp. 40–42.

8

Organizational Developments: Escalating Confrontation

See there's a lot of things that take place before '84, there's ten years of education, ten years of doing other things that were connected to the anti-apartheid struggle.[1]

—**Leo Robinson, San Francisco longshoreman and anti-apartheid activist**

But I think that there were some other key, intervening events, or processes — the anti-war movement was one, I think that the '84 Jesse Jackson campaign was a big factor, too, because I think that Rainbow Coalition which he put together, rather tenuously, but it did last for a minute, brought together a lot of people who maybe hadn't worked together before. And the Free South Africa movement, for example, which was a broader extrapolation of the anti-apartheid movement, really did involve Asians and Hispanics and women's groups, who maybe had only worked together on some Jesse Rainbow issues.[2]

—**Cecilie Counts, Washington, D.C., activist**

Studies of U.S. policy toward South Africa often refer to the establishment of the Free South Africa Movement in autumn 1984 as the breakthrough in anti-apartheid protest.[3] The burst of activism surrounding the FSAM increased the movement's public visibility and coincided with a general strategy of presenting apartheid as inimical to American identity and national interest. This section explores how anti-apartheid organizations supplied a frame through which policymakers and the public could focus, interpret, and respond to political disturbances in South Africa. Sylvia Hill explains:

The debate had always been framed in terms of communism here in the United States, that there was a need to support the regime because this was an expansion of communism for the ANC or any other group to assume state power. Well, when we framed that demonstration in that way, in terms of black people protesting, you know, in support of other black people, the next thing we knew, [this] group of Republicans, and among them, by the way, Newt Gingrich, wrote this letter to the Reagan administration saying well, we don't want to look like we're racists. Because now, being in support of apartheid was equal to being racist, you know. But that wasn't anything that we had logically thought through, as such. In that sense, it emerged because of the history of racism in this country. And so it worked in favor of shifting, shifting the way the struggle was talked about. We no longer had to try to defeat the notion that the liberation of, the dismantling of, apartheid would be equal to becoming a Communist state. Now, they had to defend how is support of that regime not being in support of racism.[4]

David A. Snow and Robert D. Benford contend that framing represents one of the most significant activities of social movements. They use the term to explain how movements "assign meaning to and interpret relevant events and conditions in ways that are intended to mobilize potential adherents and constituents, to garner bystander support, and to demobilize antagonists."[5] Framing consists of three elements: (1) diagnosis, or identification of a problem, and assigning causality; (2) prognosis, or offering a remedy, and specifying strategies, tactics and targets; and (3) motivational rationale, or a justification for engaging in collective action. This provides a useful mechanism for exploring anti-apartheid mobilization as reflected in organizational literature, congressional hearings, and popular media.

Activism produced selective campus, state, and local agency divestment in the early 1980s but had little effect on change at the federal level. Opinions varied about how to assess this. Gail Hovey, research director of the ACOA, viewed the Reagan administration as the chief obstacle to extending sanctions and favored concentration of resources on broadening anti-apartheid's public constituency. "Our feeling right now is that you can't change policy in Washington with the Reagan administration there. Although we can work on passing some bills," Hovey opined, "the basic thrust of U.S. policy is pretty horrific. The way to change that is a hard long-term process of building up a constituency across the country that will demand a different kind of policy. That's why the state and local initiatives are so important.[6]

TransAfrica's Randall Robinson concurred but held to the prospects of a Democratic victory as a conduit for policy change.

I don't think there's any point in wasting a lot of time talking about Ronald Reagan. We know we have seen put together in these four years the most anti-African policy that this country has had since World War II. But let us take our time to send a message to the Democratic Party. Let us alert the

Democratic nominee that while he may lose to Ronald Reagan with our support, he cannot hope to defeat Ronald Reagan without our support.[7]

Other movement leaders expressed optimism about the prospects for advancing anti-apartheid concerns in the 1984 elections. Jean Sindab, director of the Washington Office on Africa, considered the election opportunity "a watershed in determining U.S. policy toward southern Africa in the eighties."[8] WOA published *Election 1984: Stop U.S. Support for Apartheid,* a guide for organizers that included a list of questions for voters to pose to candidates about South Africa. The Iowa caucus efforts of the Southern Africa program of the American Friends Service Committee sought to inject apartheid into the presidential campaign. Program coordinator Jerry Herman explained that AFSC "tried to develop a constituency that was knowledgeable, but more importantly wanted to do

Randall Robinson, one of the leaders of the Free South Africa Movement, at the South African embassy, 1985. The FSAM emerged as a short-term strategy but evolved into the focal point of U.S. activism for nearly two years.

SOURCE: *Africa News,* April 1985.

something about South Africa." Herman felt that these efforts expanded public expectations about the candidates: "After we'd been through, the people in Iowa felt that they had this issue under control and that the candidates, for the most part, did not."[9] Jesse Jackson's entrance into the presidential race further assisted anti-apartheid activism, and his electoral constituency forced other Democratic candidates to clarify their positions on divestment.[10]

Despite these overtures, activists failed to push apartheid to center stage in the 1984 elections. Democratic primary candidates were reluctant to address it, and Walter Mondale's lackluster campaign against Reagan left little room for even remotely divisive issues. The coalition of anti-apartheid forces nevertheless capitalized on the opportunity to reach out to diverse constituencies. According to WOA's Sindab: "I won't even try to talk to unemployed people about what is happening 10,000 miles away unless I can make it truly relevant to what is going on in their lives. We can't approach someone who has been working on an assembly line all day the same way we talk to someone who spends the whole day studying these issues."[11]

Two events—constitutional reforms in South Africa and Reagan's reelection—indirectly gave anti-apartheid organizations a chance to exploit shifts in the opportunity structure. South Africa's reforms, exhibited as a democratic gesture, amplified the contrast between the institutional machinery available for dealing with race there and in the United States, respectively. Reagan's landslide victory, presumed to epitomize the democratic process, obscured the administration's eagerness to relegate race and human rights to the policymaking periphery. Although Pretoria's basic intransigence offered violent resistance as the only recourse for challengers, in the United States, some democratic machinery remained at the disposal of dissidents. Anti-apartheid groups exploited this to frame apartheid in ways that selectively lifted its anti-Communist shield to enhance the credibility of sanctions as a policy option.

Like NSSM-39 a decade earlier, constructive engagement helped antiapartheid groups to publicly identify those responsible for U.S. collusion with the brutal South African regime. Reagan officials tried to deflect attention from Pretoria's anachronistic and racist institutions and turn it toward the specter of Soviet-backed intervention. From this perspective, challenges to the South African state, whether from the ANC, the UDF, or popular demands for majority rule, constituted radical changes that threatened national interests. This aggressive, anti-Communist defense of Pretoria accelerated the movement's shift from moral suasion to more explicit political analysis.

In a variety of forums, movement groups portrayed apartheid as a political cancer eroding American ideals of justice and fairness. Going beyond simply labeling Reagan officials racist, activists linked the administration to a South African state seeking to draw the United States into its web of pathologies. TransAfrica's Randall Robinson, for example, called attention to Reagan's recognition of Soviet political prisoner Andrei Sakharov and his refusal to accord Nelson Mandela the same status. Whereas Crocker stressed the importance of sensitivity to white South African needs, University of Pittsburgh professor Dennis Brutus, a black South African exile, reminded audiences that apartheid relied "on violence and deprivation of basic human and civil rights."[12]

The White House tried to undermine the sanctions drive by recounting the purported benefits of maintaining a corporate presence in South Africa. Administration officials claimed that U.S. investments contributed to the modernization of South Africa's economy, thereby rendering racial segregation obsolete. They argued that counterproductive sanctions would impose additional hardships on blacks and maintained that working quietly with the Botha government instead of criticizing it increased the administration's leverage for encouraging reform. Policymakers retained the fiction that American capital was a beacon of light, that contact with Washington would restrain Pretoria's aberrant behavior.

In stark contrast to administration emphasis on capital's potential to modernize and humanize apartheid, activist critiques focused on Pretoria's mobilization of capital to preserve racial segregation. Under the circumstances, applying economic pressure represented corrective action. David Hauck of the Investor Responsibility Research Center testified about the potential impact of sanctions before a congressional subcommittee. Hauck distinguished between American commercial and manufacturing firms operating on the periphery of the South African economy and the more strategic roles that foreign capital and technology played in animating the apartheid system. James Cason, editor of *Southern Africa Magazine*, asserted that sanctions "would especially damage the strategic sectors of the South African economy where reliance on outside technology and know-how is so great."[13] WOA's Sindab questioned Reagan's eagerness to use sanctions against Libya and Nicaragua, but not South Africa. Randall Robinson pointed to the shortsightedness of administrative efforts to discourage sanctions: "The struggle in South Africa is not for better American conduct in the workplace. The struggle is for enfranchisement, the restoration of their birthright, a dismantlement of apartheid and full participation of all South Africans, on a one-person, one-vote basis."[14]

This direct political challenge to constructive engagement in the mid-1980s was accompanied by a cultural boycott movement that helped create support for the use of sanctions. The cultural boycott could clearly explain apartheid's connection to American life and could provide opportunities for the expression of popular opposition. Efforts concentrated on discouraging attendance at performances endorsed or sponsored by the South African state or preventing their occurrence. American audiences needed to know how support for such entertainment and sports unwittingly helped sanitize apartheid.

The message was conveyed through a variety of media, including music. Among the most successful was the music video *Sun City*, which portrayed popular rhythm-and-blues, rock, and rap artists rejecting invitations to lend legitimacy to the apartheid state. *Sun City* was distributed as a package, including an album, a book, and a guide for teaching about apartheid. Barbara Masekela, ANC secretary for culture, reacted favorably to this innovation:

> As Artists United Against Apartheid through the *Sun City* project, they said loudly and clearly, "I ain't gonna play Sun City." The people of South Africa and anti-apartheid supporters the world over said, "More power." We cheer Steven Van Zandt and his fellow artists because they are unequivocally declaring where they stand in the fight against the latter-day Nazis of South Africa. We cheer because they are exposing the obscenity of Sun City built in the midst of apartheid-made hunger, suffering, repression, torture and death.[15]

Like any foreign policy issue that lacked an immediate or identifiable military threat, sanctions faced considerable obstacles in furnishing a justification for collective action. Traditional assumptions discouraged citizen involvement in foreign affairs. Anti-apartheid activists also confronted Reagan administration claims that geopolitical realities and commitments must moderate the desire to force change on South Africa. Reagan officials wished the public to believe that sanctions served primarily a rhetorical purpose, because South Africa's natural resources and advanced industrial economy made it self-sufficient and thus immune to external pressures. Activists countered White House constructions of apartheid by representing it as a system connected to problems much closer to home, such as political instability in Central America and domestic structural unemployment.

Several tours organized by anti-apartheid groups demonstrate how this was done. During May 1984, the ACOA, the WOA, and Lutheran World Ministries organized a tour to advance the state divestment drive in Ohio and link apartheid with growing industrial unemployment in the United States. Participants held discussions with churches, labor unions, investors clubs, and other organizations to develop strategies for breaking local links to apartheid. These departures led to the formation of Ohio Divest, a statewide coordinating committee.[16]

Columbia University students demonstrating outside the renamed "Mandela Hall," 1985. Although the demonstrations ended after three weeks, trustees of the university voted for divestment in September 1985.

SOURCE: *Africa News*, May 1985.

A second, more extensive tour in spring 1986 showed that movement organizations could confidently convey messages in ways that reduced the traditional distinctions between domestic and foreign policy concerns. The Africa Peace Tour covered eleven states and thirty-one cities over a three-week period. It concentrated on Indiana, Kansas, and Florida, states with legislators on key congressional committees that exercised influence on African policy. Organizers hoped to:

1. draw public attention in the U.S. to the ways in which warfare and militarization are major obstacles to combating famine and hunger, refugees and debt,
2. demonstrate ways in which Americans can counteract militaristic policies toward Africa,
3. provide Americans with knowledge of the history of exploitation of Africa,

4. show the role that the U.S. plays in southern Africa,
5. build support for human rights,
6. show connections between militarization in Africa and poverty, job loss and economic uncertainty in the U.S., and
7. help build and strengthen connections among existing anti-hunger, peace, development and human rights advocacy groups and strengthen their capacity to combat militarization.[17]

The tours illustrated the increased willingness of movement groups to take risks in challenging administration efforts to invalidate the sanctions strategy. The campaigns could deepen anti-apartheid connections to more familiar political issues—racial discrimination, political repression and violence, and the anxieties associated with intervention in foreign conflicts—or they could offend constituencies reluctant to abandon traditional notions of Africa as exotic and extraneous. The longer such public concern about apartheid could be sustained, the greater the prospects for achieving linkage.

The Free South Africa Movement as Political Theater

In the mid-1980s, the FSAM dominated media coverage of domestic anti-apartheid protests. Scholarly treatments of FSAM attribute this to its resemblance to civil rights organizations of two decades earlier.[18] Such a correspondence neglects important factors that enlisted America's conflicted racial past as a weapon in the anti-apartheid struggle. It would seem that a more productive way of understanding the rise of FSAM and its collateral demonstrations is to view them as political theater. Scholars such as E. P. Thompson and Clifford Geertz have demonstrated the value of interpreting politics in theatrical terms, or as symbol-laden performances whose efficacy lies primarily in the power to move audiences beyond the spaces where they are ordinarily prepared to go.[19] This approach seems ideally suited for analysis of anti-apartheid protests at the South African embassy and its consulates around the country. As nonviolent demonstrations that posed no direct physical or economic threat to the Reagan administration or the South African government, the protests derived their power almost exclusively from their potency as performances that could symbolically undermine the legitimacy of the cooperation between the Washington and Pretoria and thereby press larger audiences and constituencies into action.

To characterize FSAM as theater is not simply to label it "playacting." Although theater works from a familiar script, with occasional improvisation, it can be viewed as a strategy that unfolds against a background of political rituals or traditional cultural ceremonies and performances that serve to confirm existing hierarchical relations and uphold the status quo.[20] In their study of Chinese politics, Joseph W. Esherick and Jeffrey N. Wasserstrom define political theater as that which "expresses beliefs about the proper distribution and disposition of power (defined broadly, or in a 'Foucaldian' sense) and other scarce resources. Unlike political rituals, which in our limited definition always perform a hegemonic function of confirming power relations, political theater often challenges or subverts the authority (or in E. P. Thompson's phrase, 'twists the tail') of ruling elites."[21]

The power of political theater lies in its potential to subvert state rituals or to capture the stage on which the state performs its rituals. After seizing the stage, challenging performers improvise their scripts to expose the follies of tradition, mock ruling elites, or call attention to the suffering of silenced victims. Performances serve as catalysts in affecting the participants, who deepen their level of commitment to the cause; the authorities, who can respond, ignore, or repress demonstrators; and the attentive public, which through television and other media connects with protests and indirectly places pressure on the authorities.

This method is especially appropriate for analyzing FSAM, for considering Reagan's revitalization of ritual as an element of political power, and for assessing the traditional conduct of foreign policy as a ritualized, expert-dominated, privatized process. Since his 1981 inauguration, Reagan ritualized virtually every aspect of his presidency, from press conferences to First Family vacations.[22] Administration foreign policy combined resumption of the use of military force to restore national power and prestige with rhetoric that characterized popular revolts against right-wing authoritarian regimes as threats to the national interest. One of Reagan's most effective public relations triumphs resulted from the invasion of tiny Grenada. The urgency that attended each of these foreign policy episodes contributed to attenuating public debate and concealed deeper patterns of corruption that linked the administration to unsavory elements in Central America, southern Africa, and the Middle East.[23]

The relative calm of postelection rituals in Washington, D.C., contrasted sharply with the violence unleashed by Pretoria's cosmetic constitutional revisions. The FSAM launched its public phase in this temporary serenity. TransAfrica staffer Cecilie Counts describes the circumstances that provoked a new strategy:

[O]ur response was triggered by those terrible incidents in '84 when they sent those troops into the townships, so, again, Richard Hatcher, who was mayor of Gary, Indiana, and, at that time, chairman of the board of TransAfrica, they basically said to Randall Robinson, "We have to do something, we've done the lobbying, we've done the picket lines, we've done the white house, we've done the candlelight vigil, we've got to do something else." So we really went to the stage of daily demonstrations at the embassy and all of that out of desperation, frustration with traditional lobbying. We were never going to be the Christian Coalition or these big right-wing think tanks that were starting to come up during the Reagan years. Human Events and all these other far right groups with the money and the resources—we could never match that. We weren't even successfully keeping our fingers in the dikes. So, when it came to South Africa and our degree of desperation we said, "To the streets!"[24]

TransAfrica played a key role in creating the FSAM, but protest activities included a broad coalition of activists, elected officials, labor unions, and student, civil rights, and church groups that orchestrated a series of well-publicized arrests outside the South African embassy and at its consulates around the United States. Just as in theater—which creates a dialogue between the audience and actors, who use shortcuts or familiar themes to convey messages—the day, the target, and the setting all contained symbolic value that helped protesters appropriate the stage of public opinion. In this case, demonstrations began on Friday, November 23, the day after Thanksgiving, when the traditional opening of the Christmas shopping season dominated national and local news. The delivery of a petition directly to the South African Embassy, symbolically bypassing conventional diplomats, appealed to Pretoria to respect the human rights of nonwhites. It drew attention, during a season of conspicuous consumption—and glut—in America, to the deprivation experienced by Africans in the republic. The evocation of powerful cultural symbols was meant to elicit a sympathetic response from media and the American public.

To TransAfrica member Willard Johnson, the timing of the FSAM was critical. "The demonstrations have ventilated a lot of frustrated concerns, given the reversals, the disappointments and disasters associated with Reagan's first term," he explained. "Then came more frustrations through an election campaign that failed to give sufficient consideration to the South African issue, despite Jesse Jackson's valiant efforts to raise it, and catalytic events in South Africa itself, which called for response."[25]

The unfolding drama in the capital invidiously compared national progress on race relations to South Africa's reluctance to abandon its anachronistic institutions. The District of Columbia, once one of the nation's most segregated cities, in 1984 had elected its second black mayor, former civil rights activist Marion Barry, and recently battled the Republican-dominated Senate over the legality of the city's divestment decisions. A *New Republic* article captured the ritualistic element of the demonstrations: "Everyday the drill on Massachusetts Avenue is the same. The picketers arrive around 3:30, and after a half hour Randall Robinson steps to the microphone set up on the lawn in front of the empty chateau. 'Will the designated messengers of the day please assemble behind the lectern,' he will say, and then he introduces them."[26] The humane treatment accorded demonstrators by district police called attention to the way the historic civil rights movement had transformed arrest procedures. The scripts also provided powerful enticement for television news and offered numerous local perspectives on a breaking national and international issue.[27]

The embassy performance was duplicated in other cities as demonstrators targeted South African consulates and eventually produced complementary theatrical venues—"shantytowns"—on college campuses. The construction of shanties sometimes occasioned hostile responses from local police or divestment opponents, who destroyed the structures—only to see them reconstructed the next day. As a result, demonstrators effectively drew opponents into symbolic reenactment of the violence of the South African state.[28]

The power of theater did not rest in its ability to communicate truth about violence and injustice in South Africa but implicated the Reagan administration in Pretoria's cruelty. Relying upon the code of expertise, the administration rationalized its patience with the Botha government by invoking Cold War claims about South Africa's importance to national security. By contrast, the FSAM used scripts familiar to domestic audiences to make the case that sanctions were the logical step if the United States was to distance itself from the South African government.

The effectiveness of theater also drew on its public nature, which stood in direct contrast to the secrecy of constructive engagement. Petitioning the South African government was a call to open up the political process to previously excluded groups. Sylvia Hill, an FSAM steering committee member, explained how the demography of protest also reflected its ideals. "Not only is the movement multiracial and multidenominational, but there is also political and ideological diversity. Different sectors of the American people are becoming involved, at least at the physical level, to show some kind of viable option to apartheid."[29]

All citizens were invited to participate. Over a five-month period, more than 3,000 demonstrators were arrested in Washington, D.C., and more than 4,000 in protests in twenty-six other cities and college campuses, including twenty-two members of Congress, several mayors, and union and religious leaders.[30] Counts describes the ripple effect:

> There were so many angry people anyway, who had been stepped on by Reagan, and then there were remnants of this Jesse coalition with nothing to

do out there, so that when we said to people, "Okay, you don't have to come to Washington to demonstrate at the embassy, you can go to your local Krugerrand retailer in Des Moines, or you can go to the passport office in Chicago—pick a symbolic target." Well, there were these local little coalitions that—at least, there were phone trees left or whatever that anti-apartheid activists could use in their communities to sort of replicate what we were doing.[31]

The decision to highlight the arrests of prominent people disturbed long-time activists, but according to TransAfrica's David Scott, the celebrity presence assured media coverage and legitimized the movement in the eyes of viewers unfamiliar with its goals and objectives. "The purpose is never to exclude anyone, but to include people who never have been involved in anti-apartheid activities before and had never participated in an act of civil disobedience. The question is how do you bring those people in? And at least part of the answer is to get people like Senator Lowell Weicker and Coretta Scott King and the Kennedys involved."[32] Counts elaborated further on the instrumental value of celebrity:

[E]minently respectable people went first. So that, by the time that regular people started going, (a) the police knew that this was a sustained action, they were going to have to deal with this every day, and the South African government knew it and the State Department knew it, and (b) they had to face the prospect of actually prosecuting in front of a D.C. jury, Stevie Wonder, and Harry Belafonte, and Senator Lowell Weicker and members of the Congressional Black Caucus before they got to Joe Blow. Which is why I think they made the decision to start dropping those charges. Because by that time we had all these high-powered lawyers lined up to defend us and a media campaign that would have backed it up and we were ready for a trial—"Try us." They didn't want to do this, Robert Kennedy's kids, they'd have to do them first.[33]

The duration and intensity of the demonstrations confirmed participant willingness to pursue the public good in an era of rampant individualism. *Time* magazine reported that "for more than eight months now, through winter freeze and summer swelt, scores of Americans, black and white, have been assembling in front of the large sand-colored South African embassy on Massachusetts Avenue in Washington to demonstrate their revulsion from apartheid."[34] In short, FSAM appealed to a tradition of principled dissent that U.S. policymakers had validated less than two decades earlier with civil rights legislation and had consecrated less than two years before with the 1983 creation of the Martin Luther King Jr. holiday. Sylvia Hill discussed FSAM's endurance and appeal:

William Gray, who led the fight for sanctions in the House of Representatives. Gray's leadership reflected the strategic positions occupied by senior members of the Congressional Black Caucus.

SOURCE: *Africa News*, April 1985.

It grew on its own up until the cold winter months, up until January or February. And then it picked back up again, actually, in the spring, for a while as well. So churches, church denominations certainly had, you know, there were busloads of people who came from Indiana and different states that would come, who had never, never demonstrated before. Which was rather interesting in and of itself. I mean, you had to show them how to walk around the line and so forth. So, it took off—there were, you know, increasingly more diverse groups, like Lawyers Against Apartheid, Psychologists Against Apartheid, social workers, the Fifth Street Baptist Church Against Apartheid, even one day there was a very popular tavern that's near Catholic University that is not purely student but it's also a workers' organization, and this whole Happy Hour group came, I mean these people had organized this and they, it meant something to them. I mean, you had those kinds of experiences to the one woman, who I remember, who was a very old woman and she came and she walked back and she came, and she said to me, she said, "I tried all my life to never go to jail. This is very hard for me because I tried to be a good person, you know." And I could just talk to her about, she says, "I just don't feel like it's right there and I want to show that, I don't agree with it, you know." So, the symbol of it I think, resonated with people in terms of their own personal consciousness. Though, activists, many left activists said this is just getting to be melodramatic, its just phony, its not really a protest, but it meant a lot to a lot of people who saw themselves, I guess, as mainstream and hardworking people, but they saw this as a way of expressing their discontent.[35]

Evidence of Consciousness-Raising

Apartheid had acquired a level of public salience by the mid-1980s that enabled activists to sustain protest drives but also propelled them to take risks with the potential to extend the range and depth of the movement. An abundance of evidence—media coverage, public opinion polls, public- and private-sector disengagement from South Africa, and congressional reluctance to allow Reagan to regain control of policy responses toward apartheid—signaled shifts in the political opportunity structure that warranted such optimism.

An explosion of media coverage seconded movement claims about the brutality of apartheid. Television network news programs and special reports presented a steady flow of information on South African unrest, Reagan's response, and domestic protest activities.[36] The spread of protest to local communities presented network affiliates with opportunities to link regional business and religious news to South Africa's turmoil. These developments made it possible for organizations to redirect resources away from basic information provision (Figure 8.1).

Substantial growth in public support for movement objectives occurred from 1977 to 1985–1986. A September 1985 Gallup poll revealed that 47 percent of respondents felt that the government should place more pressure on South Africa. Fifteen percent favored less, and 37 percent felt that no change in the amount of pressure was necessary. Asked the same question a year later, 55 percent wanted more pressure on Pretoria, 14 percent wanted less, and 24 percent approved of the current level.[37]

By the end of 1986, 21 states, 68 cities, and 10 of the nation's largest counties had adopted divestment policies. Over 100 educational institutions had withdrawn nearly $500 million from companies profiting from apartheid. U.S. investments in South Africa totaled $2.8 billion in 1983 but by 1985 had decreased to $1.3 billion. Some 350 American corporations operated in South Africa in 1984. Eighty of them, including GM, IBM, Coca-Cola, Xerox, Eastman Kodak, Honeywell, Exxon, and Mc-

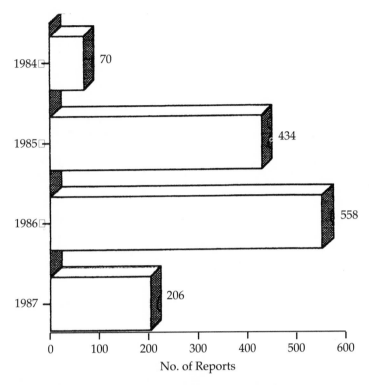

FIGURE 8.1   Television Network News Coverage of South Africa, 1984–1987

SOURCE: *Television News Index and Abstracts* (Nashville, Tenn.: Vanderbilt Television News Archives, 1984–1987).

Graw-Hill, had pulled out by 1987 (Figure 8.2). Dramatic increases in external support and improved internal resources propelled the anti-apartheid movement toward the center of the domestic political stage.[38]

Besides performing the hard work that led to enactment of the Comprehensive Anti-Apartheid Act of 1986, anti-apartheid activists gained gratification from bringing together diverse groups of people to explore the options available for challenging a popular president. Willard Johnson explained the feelings of efficacy generated during this stage of activism: "It's really a social movement," he averred. "It encompasses the divestment campaign, the cultural boycott, the students. True, the movement has an organizational character, but it acts as a wedge into the public consciousness, giving the public events in which they can participate as demonstrators and the media news they can cover."[39]

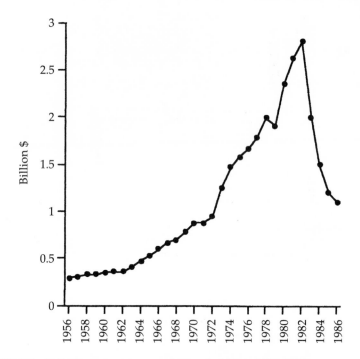

FIGURE 8.2   U.S. Direct Investments in South Africa, 1956–1986

SOURCE: Richard W. Hull, *American Enterprise in South Africa* (New York: NYU Press, 1990), 369–370.

Conclusion

From 1984 through 1986, political unrest in South Africa and the inability of the Reagan administration to mollify critics of its relations with the republic created a cluster of actionable issues—the escalation of township violence, increased state repression, the declaration of a state emergency, the disrespect shown to Nobel Laureate Desmond Tutu—that enabled the anti-apartheid movement to focus on separating American public- and private-sector institutions from apartheid. Deterioration and uncertainty in South Africa eroded support for the administration's position in both houses of Congress, within the corporate community, and among a broad range of strategically important domestic constituencies. The climate gave activists the opportunity to experiment and to expand their action repertoire, thus offering a broader range of social and expressive benefits to newly mobilized constituencies, seasoned supporters, and the general public.

Notes

1. Leo Robinson, interview by Billy Nessen, Clarity Film Productions, Berkeley, 1996, p. 4.

2. Cecilie Counts, interview by Connie Field, Clarity Film Productions, Berkeley, 1996, p. 8.

3. Les de Villiers, *In Sight of Surrender: The U.S. Sanctions Campaign Against South Africa, 1946–1993* (New York: Praeger, 1995), pp. 83–84.

4. Sylvia Hill, interview by Connie Field, Clarity Film Productions, Berkeley, 1996, p. 14.

5. David A. Snow and Robert D. Benford, "Ideology, Frame Resonance, and Participant Mobilization," in *International Social Movement Research,* vol. 1 (Greenwich, Conn.: JAI Press, 1988), p. 197.

6. Michael Maren, "The Africa Lobby: Building a Constituency Against Apartheid," *Africa Report* 29, 3 (May–June 1984):55.

7. "Black Lobby Asks Democrats to Put Africa on Agenda," *Africa News* 23, 1–2 (July 16, 1984):1.

8. Maren, "The Africa Lobby," p. 57.

9. Ibid., p. 57.

10. Lorenzo Morris and Linda F. Williams, "The Coalition at the End of the Rainbow: The Jackson Campaign," in Lucius J. Barker and Ronald W. Walters, eds., *Jesse Jackson's 1984 Presidential Campaign: Challenge and Change in American Politics* (Urbana: University of Illinois Press, 1989), p. 241.

11. Maren, "The Africa Lobby," p. 58.

12. Randall Robinson, "Victims of Ignorance, Too," *New York Times,* August 31, 1984; U.S. Congress, House, Committee on Foreign Affairs, Subcommittee on Africa, *South Africa Legislation, Hearings,* 98th Cong., 2d sess., April 10, August 1, and September 6, 1984.

13. "Sanctions: From the Symbolic to the Economic," *Congressional Quarterly Weekly Report* 43, 10 (March 9, 1985):446.

14. *New York Times,* April 14, 1985.

15. Barbara Masekela, "The ANC and the Cultural Boycott," *Africa Report* 32, 4 (July–August 1987):19–21.

16. Washington Office on Africa, *Washington Notes on Africa* (Spring–Summer 1984):7.

17. Washington Office on Africa, *Report on the Africa Peace Tour* (Spring 1986):1.

18. De Villiers, *In Sight of Surrender.*

19. Clifford Geertz, *Negara: The Theatre-State in Nineteenth-Century Bali* (Princeton: Princeton University Press, 1980); E. P. Thompson, "Patrician Society, Plebeian Culture," *Journal of Social History* 7, 5 (1978):382–405; Joseph W. Esherick and Jeffrey N. Wasserstrom, "Acting Out Democracy: Political Theater in China," *Journal of Asian Studies* 49, 4 (1990):835–865.

20. Steven Luke, "Political Ritual and Social Integration," *Sociology* 9, 2 (1975):289–305.

21. Esherick and Wasserstrom, "Acting Out Democracy," p. 843.

22. James Combs, *The Reagan Range: The Nostalgic Myth in American Politics* (Bowling Green, Ohio: Bowling Green State University Press, 1993); Michael

Rogin, *Ronald Reagan: The Movie and Other Episodes in Political Demonology* (Berkeley and Los Angeles: University of California Press, 1987).

23. James M. Scott, *Deciding to Intervene: The Reagan Doctrine and American Foreign Policy* (Durham, N.C.: Duke University Press, 1996), pp. 124–126.

24. Counts, interview, p. 10.

25. "Apartheid Foes Redouble Efforts," *Africa News* 24, 10 (May 20, 1985):7.

26. Nicholas von Hoffman, "Under Arrest," *New Republic* 192 (February 11, 1985):11–14.

27. David D. Newsum, *The Public Dimension of Foreign Policy* (Bloomington: Indiana University Press, 1996), pp. 96–97.

28. "Anti-Apartheid Actions Spread," *Africa News* 23 (April 21, 1986):3.

29. "Apartheid Foes Redouble Efforts," p. 8.

30. Stephen Engleberg, "Thousands Join in Protest in Washington," *New York Times*, April 21, 1985; Barry Sussman, "Activists Stimulate South Africa Sanctions," *Washington Post* July 24, 1985.

31. Counts, interview, pp. 11–12.

32. "Apartheid Foes Redouble Efforts," p. 9.

33. Counts, interview, p. 11.

34. "Principle of Vital Importance," *Time* (August 5, 1985):33.

35. Hill, interview, p. 12.

36. Danny Schecter, "South Africa: Where Did the Story Go? *Africa Report* 33, 2 (1988):27.

37. *Gallup Report* 240 (October 1985):20 and 254 (November 1986):19.

38. Paul Lansing and Sarosh Kuruvilla, "Business Divestment in South Africa: In Whose Best Interest?" *Journal of Business Ethics* 7, 8 (August 1988):564; Janice Love, "The Potential Impact of Sanctions Against South Africa," *Journal of Modern African Studies* 26, 1 (March 1988):103; Eric L. Hirsch "Sacrifice for the Cause: Group Processes, Recruitment, and Commitment in a Student Social Movement," *American Sociological Review* 55 (April 1990):246–252.

39. "Apartheid Foes Redouble Efforts," p. 7.

9

Conclusion

For nearly a century, U.S. society displayed little concern for the institutionalized racial oppression that evolved into apartheid. Sporadic incidents in South Africa drove home the incompatibility between that nation's racialist ideology and American democratic principles, but pro-apartheid interest groups dominated the foreign policymaking process. Flashes of hope accompanied the new post–World War II international consensus on abhorrence of political systems based on racial discrimination and denial of basic human rights. The first wave of African independence movements during the 1950s signaled a rapid end to colonialism. Yet for the next thirty years, Washington officials, citing the dangers of Soviet aggression and premature African independence, resisted citizen group claims that apartheid compromised American principles and endangered the long-term interests of the United States.

Explaining the Shift in U.S. Foreign Policy Response

How did policymakers reach a consensus on recognizing sanctions as an appropriate mechanism for pressuring South Africa to dismantle its racial separatist system? The consensus resulted from a grudging acceptance by major institutional decisionmakers of the need to distance themselves from apartheid. The intensity and duration of mid-1980s antiapartheid activism make it tempting to attribute movement influence to specific episodes, agents, or institutional responses. Mobilization against apartheid cannot be separated, however, from transformations experienced in the United States throughout the 1960s and 1970s that profoundly shaped which groups got organized and how they did so. A flood of movements—promoting civil rights or the rights of women, ethnic groups, farm workers, gay people, or seniors; pro-environment, antiwar, antinuclear, and so on—drove formerly marginalized groups into conventional political arenas to introduce broad reforms.[1] The peak of this activist surge coincided with the early growth stages of apartheid as a policy problem, consequently shaping the environment that movements sought to influence.

Popular movements capitalized on a series of favorable economic, social, and political trends that sustained and intensified the climate for questioning the dominant institutions that held sway over the relatively complacent 1950s.[2] Long-term economic growth enlarged the middle class and increased its discretionary income. The maturing baby boom generation supplied a steady stream of entrants into diverse yet potentially mobilizable spaces in the consumer marketplace, the workforce, and higher education. Lower voter turnout paradoxically accompanied rising issue-oriented, independent voting. Nonelectoral political activity abetted social movement activism. Governmental program expansion in areas from economic development to social services increased the range of administrators, groups, claimants, and public interest and media guardians in the political arena. Gradual changes in the composition of American politics and the expectations of participants sharpened the focus on critical junctures such as the Vietnam War and the Watergate scandal. These provided windows on the limitations of mainstream institutional responses to the fundamental problems that threatened the material well-being of significant sectors of society as well as established notions of ethical public behavior.

These primarily domestic manifestations do not fully explain the political climate that enlarged the public's capacity to respond to an expanding array of divisive foreign policy issues. By the mid-1970s, American society faced the energy crisis and economic instability in what Anthony Giddens refers to as "world time," or shared cross-national experiences that illuminate how actions taken in one country have rapid effects elsewhere.[3] Disruptions imposed by external security commitments, dependence on imported oil, and industrial decline heightened awareness of interrelatedness. Daily experiences of entertainment, travel, educational exchange, and news enhanced consciousness of global interdependence while raising questions about America's role in it.

Interdependence honed the salience of African issues and shaped the temporal opportunities available for activism in American politics. Peter Schraeder's analysis of three policymaking patterns in U.S. responses provides insights into how African problems penetrated the fabric of domestic politics.[4] The first involves routine situations such as diplomatic, trade, and commercial matters where policymaking is confined to those divisions of the foreign affairs bureaucracy that specialize in African affairs. A second pattern occurs when an African state faces an invasion, insurgency, or coup d'état, creating a situation in which the U.S. president and his closest advisers attempt crisis management by asserting control, establishing priorities, and setting timetables for resolution. Such occasions create actionable issues, or circumstances in which authorities must explain and respond, or risk losing legitimacy at home and abroad. A third pattern of responses emerges during extended crisis situations in which the inability of the executive branch to manage a problem causes it to spill over into domestic politics. Public discussions of the problem engage a wider range of participants, including Congress, interest groups, think tanks, media, and rank-and-file citizen organizations. Apart from multiplying the voices in public debates, contested policy issues in extended crisis situations may acquire narratives and project imagery that enable far-reaching assaults on established points of view.[5]

Few citizens concern themselves with foreign affairs on a daily basis, but prolonged crisis situations attract public attention and invite comparisons with other episodes in the nation's history. Resolution of the problem consequently grows more difficult as a multiplicity of voices addresses it. In contrast to isolated African civil wars and revolts in the 1960s, conflicts arising from southern African liberation struggles transcended Cold War containment frameworks and invited comparisons with national liberation conflicts in Southeast Asia and Central America and the civil rights movement in the United States.[6]

The Value of the Political Process Model

This study has used a political process model to guide analysis of American anti-apartheid activism. Political process offers a more comprehensive alternative to three other perspectives: classical theory, resource mobilization theory, and new social movements. Classical theory has been particularly important in the development of social movement theory, but it cannot adequately explain how anti-apartheid activism in the United States evolved during the era outlined above. Its major weakness stems from the assumption that there is a direct correspondence between levels of social tension and the appearance of aggrieved people's collective response. To classical theorists who view activism as alienated and isolated from society, social movements represent psychological rather than political responses. This study emphasizes the way anti-apartheid organizations drew on economic-social structural changes. It has also shown that participant involvement includes a range of traditional social and political activities and is not limited to anti-apartheid protests. This invalidates the distinction that classical theorists make between ordinary political behavior and collective action.

Resource mobilization theory emerged as a corrective to the classical model and contributed to the revitalization of the study of social movements. Its proponents claim that collective movements emerge when aggrieved groups receive more external social resources, making it possible for them to launch more effective organized demands for change. By focusing on the contributions of external groups, however, advocates of this model discount the significance of internal assets as factors that facilitate movement growth and development. The most obvious deficiency in applying this perspective to the anti-apartheid movement is that it unduly emphasizes mainstream allies and institutions. It overlooks the roles played by popular organizations, especially ad hoc groups.

New social movement theory offers some insights into how groups form in advanced industrial societies and how they develop expanded action repertoires for politicizing grievances. But there is little or no evidence implying that anti-apartheid activism represents a fundamental break from dominant values in American society. The organizational base of the anti-apartheid movement, in any case, defies neat ideological categorization.

In contrast to previous models, the revised political process perspective that guided this study is based on the premise that intense levels of globalization shape the frequency and intensity of U.S. interactions with Africa and the probability that those encounters will trigger domestic responses that link apartheid to problems and concerns familiar to American society. This implies that political process evolves beyond established state routines and structures and includes expectations associated with complex international involvement rather than with single events. Ongoing adjustment to global interdependence destabilized efforts to uphold Cold War–derived dichotomies between First World and Third World, between causes and effects, and between "us" and "them."

The intent of this study has not been to recount the complete history of anti-apartheid activism.[7] Instead, drawing from available evidence, it has used a political process model to illustrate how the movement evolved during a period of fundamental national and global change. The central argument has been that the rise of the anti-apartheid movement is best explained by three factors singled out by the political process model. First, the political opportunity structure improved as fixed international and domestic relationships became more vulnerable to criticism. Second, organizations capitalized on social and economic structural changes to refine efforts to recruit new members, create resources, develop alliances, and expand the repertoire of protest techniques. Last, movement confidence grew as smaller, sometimes symbolic victories achieved at the state and local level indirectly forced major financial, educational, and governmental institutions to alter their routine, uncritical ways of dealing with South Africa.

The 1960 Sharpeville massacre of unarmed demonstrators occurred during a period of heightened domestic and international concern about

African independence, but the overall political climate did not support a vital anti-apartheid movement in the United States. Groups that lacked organizational resources and political seasoning also faced a political sensibility that provided few instruments for interpreting African conflicts beyond the dominant Cold War containment framework. Pervasive anticommunism reinforced assumptions about Pretoria's value to U.S. national security and encouraged further ties to South Africa over the next decade. These obstacles nevertheless galvanized the Africanist constituency to move away from its primarily cultural and information-provision orientation.

In contrast to the 1960s, when South African–American relations seemed immune to international anti-apartheid interventionist efforts, opportunities for disrupting that exclusivity improved in the early 1970s as both countries experienced deeper penetration by external economic and political forces. The slow, agonizing closure of the Vietnam era by 1975 left in its wake an assertive Congress, a weakened presidency, enclaves of politicized citizen groups, and unresolved questions about the direction of foreign policy. High rates of inflation and unemployment and uncertainty about the country's energy resources and the environment reinforced public skepticism about political leadership and ethics.

South Africa's further integration into the global economy similarly challenged that nation's sense of self-reliance and its mechanisms of political control. Industrial expansion simultaneously entailed greater dependency on imported capital and technology and skilled black labor. Yet each of these inputs increased the potential disruption of the racial system. The shortage of white workers led Pretoria to accept more "illegal" black migration into officially segregated urban areas, thus indirectly contributing to the politicization of black trade unions. The 1975 collapse of southern Africa's white buffer states forced South Africa to divert substantial resources from economic modernization to defense.

Anti-apartheid activists sensitive to global trends attempted to synchronize accounts of how the world political economy was being restructured with explanations of the American role in southern Africa. They tried to marshal public skepticism, memory, and experience against the Ford administration's bid to effect a Vietnam-style intervention in Angola's civil war and Washington's anachronistic construction of South Africa's strategic importance.

Southern Africa in the second half of the 1970s was a magnet for great power rivalry. Its prominence in the news coincided with post-Watergate and post-Vietnam electoral and policy adjustments and sustained the visibility of apartheid as an issue in domestic politics. The violent unraveling of southern Africa's racist colonial hegemony resonated with America's conflictual racial past, thereby drawing in new sites, constituencies, targets, and analogies in policy debates and fostering linkages with peace, antinuclear, and Central American protest constituencies. A diverse set of movement groups capitalized on this energized political climate by penetrating established decisionmaking arenas with alternative policies. Movement confidence and resilience snowballed, even in the face of rising conservatism in the White House and in the Senate. The costs of mobilization declined as a result of the peculiar economy of scale that the proliferation of targets and sites, actionable issues, and media coverage provided.

The peak of anti-apartheid activism in the 1980s supported the movement's claims to more thoroughly understand public sentiment than Reagan's foreign policy experts did. Anti-apartheid groups played pivotal roles in explaining domestic linkages to the turmoil in southern Africa, focusing public attention on defects in Reagan's constructive engagement policies and outlining an array of choices for those wishing to disengage from apartheid. Activists sustained interest in the protracted South African struggle and confidently used the symbols and narratives of America's civil rights movement to force policymakers to justify their toleration of the internationally discredited apartheid regime.

Explaining the Decline of Anti-Apartheid Activism

A political process approach that uses a set of multiple factors to explain the rise of activism must remain sensitive to how those factors shape movement decline. Despite continuing unrest in South Africa and increased demands for more comprehensive sanctions, the momentum that culminated in the 1986 legislation ultimately could not be recaptured. The structure of political opportunity contracted as the state and corporate policymakers displaced the movement in responding to the seemingly intractable South African situation. The movement's broad-based consensus evaporated as issues proliferated and as new groups and strategies crowded the narrowing stage of opportunity. With the rise of competing issues—the Iran-Contra scandal, Gorbachev's reform efforts in the Soviet Union, domestic economic uncertainty, and the upcoming 1988 presidential election—the public salience of apartheid as a policy problem rapidly declined.

The intensity of protest in South Africa lasted throughout the mid-1980s. As the political atmosphere became much more complex, however, it eluded the simplistic interpretations of the struggle often made by casual external observers and the international news media. A severely weakened Pretoria still exercised influence on the balance of internal forces and international perceptions of its own instrumentality. The July 1986 declaration of a state of emergency set in motion a strategy by the Botha government that combined infrastructural improvements in black communities with greater controls on political dissent and press censorship.

State maneuvers reduced foreign news reporting and interrupted the protest momentum, exacerbating tensions within the movement as groups struggled to develop new strategies. The recognition of the ANC by more governments and the growing perception that it possessed the most solid political credentials for affecting the transition to a multiracial nation meant the displacement of the UDF as coordinator of the resistance. As the claims and agendas of such groups as the Zulu organization Inkatha, and the nationalist Azania People's Organization clashed, the state covertly exploited their differences. Lacking wider access to South African society, external news media interpreted these internecine struggles as black-on-black violence, detaching them from the ongoing battles against apartheid.[8]

Enactment of the Congressional Anti-Apartheid Act shifted the frontier of South African–American relations to congressional-executive battles over implementation and extension of sanctions.[9] Congressional liberals, recalling Reagan's unswerving opposition to punitive action against South Africa, raised concerns about provisions within the 1986 sanctions legislation that left room for discretion in enforcement. In particular, they pointed to terms within the law that permitted the president to exempt from the sanctions list "strategic" minerals deemed essential to national security. To reduce enforcement latitude, Ronald Dellums (D.–Calif.) introduced a bill into the House (HR-1580) in March 1987 that called for withdrawal of all U.S. investments from South Africa, a complete ban on trade with the regime, and prohibition of all American military and intelligence cooperation.[10] Dellums's bill, a comprehensive rather than incremental approach to disengagement, passed the House but failed to reach the Senate floor for a vote.

The Reagan administration indirectly conceded the failure of constructive engagement but yielded little ground to Congress. The White House maintained that congressional sanctions represented an addition to existing executive branch restrictions on exchange with South Africa rather than new measures. Reagan officials argued that additional sanctions would make Pretoria more obstinate and upset delicate ongoing negotiations on conflicts in Angola, Mozambique, and Namibia. Additionally, they contended that sanctions did not work alone but rather in tandem with such administration initiatives as the meetings between Secretary of State George Shultz and ANC president Oliver Tambo and State Department funding of black entrepreneurship programs in South Africa.

Administration reactions stemmed from hoping to avoid repetition of the embarrassing 1986 congressional override of the veto and from the disintegration of the coalition that brought sanctions to the national political spotlight. Congress, having delivered a blow to the president, and the Democrats, having recaptured the Senate, turned their attention to the 1988 elections. News from South Africa offered no definitive answers to the question of the effectiveness of sanctions. Lacking a sense of emergency, liberal anti-apartheid voices in both houses of Congress became increasingly isolated. Both Democratic and Republican conservatives took advantage of this respite to shift the focus to the administration's efforts to fund the UNITA anti-Marxist rebels in Angola. With no short-term benefits accruing from opposing a popular president, maneuvering for position in the upcoming primaries, or appeasing aroused constituencies back home, the congressional push for additional sanctions weakened.

Active opposition to apartheid remained a high priority for several national groups, but mobilization efforts confronted a public mood devoid of the urgency that had ignited earlier sanctions drives.[11] In March 1987, TransAfrica announced its "Faces Behind Apartheid" campaign. Its articles and advertisements in newspapers spotlighted politicians and organizations that maintained covert alliances with Pretoria. The drive's first two faces were Republican senators Robert Dole and Jesse Helms, who had been significant obstacles in the congressional sanctions debate and major supporters of Reagan's bid to fund UNITA.[12] A few months later, the Lawyers Committee for Civil Rights Under Law held a symposium at the Rayburn House Office Building to announce its new project, "Free South Africa's Children," which concentrated on fund-raising to address problems experienced by South Africa youth in the wake of massive political and economic destabilization.[13]

In the fall of 1987, ACOA coordinated a campaign called "Unlock Apartheid's Jails," which focused on the continuing plight of South African political prisoners.[14] The FSAM initiated a consumer boycott against Shell gas stations and products to protest that firm's refusal to leave South Africa. Student activists devoted considerable effort to refining links between southern African solidarity groups and organizations opposed to intervention in Central America and organizations fighting domestic racism.[15] After sanctions legislation, these diverse actions no longer seemed united by a common purpose, and few groups could sustain mobilization beyond the initial thrust. The movement's enlarged constituency had acquired what it wanted—a form of symbolic punitive action—and did not linger in a struggle that it had only recently joined. In short, the movement ended just as the T-shirts of new recruits had started to fade.

In an ironic commentary on racism, tensions between whites and nonwhites in various parts of the activist community began to erode prospects for movement rejuvenation. These strains manifested themselves in black suspicion of white paternalism, white anxiety about black anger, and black concerns about the uneven distribution of resources and staff positions in and among groups.[16] Sensitivity to these issues surfaced as the movement developed more incisive critiques of South African racial discrimination. Despite the numerous accomplishments in creating an environment in which people from different racial and cultural backgrounds could effectively cooperate, veteran Chicago anti-apartheid activist Rachel Rubin warned that "we still need to overcome the continued racial segregation within progressive, left political work and we need to continue to confront the difficulties of overcoming internalized white racism if we are really going to tackle racism in this country."[17]

The decline of anti-apartheid activism is perhaps best explained by what John Lofland characterizes as transition from a conflictual to a consensus social movement.[18] Substantial opposition to additional sanctions remained, but a consensus about the abhorrence of apartheid led many public and private sector institutions to quickly break any visible ties to Pretoria or risk public censure. No longer a source of visible domestic conflict by the summer of 1987, anti-apartheid symbols were co-opted, and to some degree, commercialized. New group formation continued, but most new organizations now had service or humanitarian aims rather than political objectives.[19] The rapid transformation of sanctions from a goal to a reality left activist groups without a well-defined strategy for advancing the struggle to a new level.

Conclusion

Analysis of the movement's decline should not overshadow its wider impact on national politics.[20] Extending beyond a mere quest for policy change, anti-apartheid activism displaced assumptions about people of African descent at home as well as abroad. It raised questions about policymaker deference to European colonial, Cold War, and corporate priorities in responding to South Africa's institutionalized violent racial order. In the course of contesting those conventions, opposition to apartheid aroused constituencies concerned with fundamental democratic problems such as how the national interest is defined and how it shapes the boundaries between foreign and domestic politics. It raised the question of who has the right to participate in foreign policy decisionmaking and to what extent civil rights and human rights considerations accompany policymaking and implementation. The movement's broad reach partly compensated for its comparative deficiencies in such conventional political resources as money, votes, and bureaucratic power.[21]

In addition to intervening in the "great conversations" that frame democratic development,[22] domestic opposition to apartheid furnished critical space for deepening inquiry into the injustices fostered by material and structural adjustments to postindustrialization. Consistent with its pre–World War II pacifist and civil rights movement origins, the movement assumed that power operates as a relationship rather than as a lever possessed by one group and unavailable to others. A relational view of power guided activists' rejection of the conventional distinctions between public and private property, thereby subjecting a range of traditional profit maximization schemes—corporate investments, pension funds, university portfolios, and so on—to moral questioning and public scrutiny. Anti-apartheid activists also identified a cluster of proximate sites and institutions—such as banks, schools, the body, consumption habits, social customs, sports, and tourism—for individuals and groups to contest American connections to southern Africa's racial order.

Last, the anti-apartheid movement injected new concerns into the political process as society experienced greater global interdependence. Outrage expressed by marginalized Americans about racial injustice in South Africa once seemed far removed from the concerns of a dominant world power, but gradually anti-apartheid activism, and other nongovernmental transnational endeavors, came to be understood as critical elements in a struggle to produce meaningful democracy in a world devoid of Cold War encumbrances. These movements may seem weak because they do not adhere to the behaviors and expectations of conventional political groups. As complex global interdependence continues to erode much of the framework ungirding the external relations of traditional state and corporate enterprises, however, the relationship between dominant institutions and transnational social movements remains potentially a very creative encounter. It is less a question of whether movements can be incorporated into established economic and governmental structures than of how movements engage the challenges of community, responsibility, democracy, equity, and violence and push them in new directions.[23]

Notes

1. Thomas Byrne Edsall, with Mary D. Edsall, *Chain Reaction: The Impact of Race, Rights, and Taxes on American Politics* (New York: W. W. Norton, 1991).

2. Marty Jezer, *The Dark Ages: Life in the United States from 1945–1960* (Boston: South End Press, 1982).

3. Anthony Giddens, *The Constitution of Society* (Berkeley and Los Angeles: University of California Press, 1984).

4. Peter J. Schraeder, *United States Foreign Policy Toward Africa: Incrementalism, Crisis, and Change* (New York: Cambridge University Press, 1994), pp. 48–50.

5. Deborah Stone, *Policy Paradox and Political Reason* (Glenview, Ill.: Scott Foresman, 1988).

6. Martin Staniland, "Africa, the American Intelligentsia, and the Shadow of Vietnam," *Political Science Quarterly* 98 (Winter 1983–1984):595–616.

7. "A History of International Anti-Apartheid Activism," forthcoming documentary film by Connie Fields, Clarity Film Productions, Berkeley.

8. Jo Ellen Fair and Roberta Astroff, "Constructing Race and Violence: U.S. News Coverage and the Signifying Practices of Apartheid," *Journal of Communications* 41, 4 (1991):58–74.

9. Linda M. Clarizio, Bradley Clements, and Erika Getter, "United States Policy Toward South Africa," *Human Rights Quarterly* 11, 2 (1989):249–294.

10. U.S. House, Subcommittees on International Economic Policy and Trade and on Africa, *Proposed Economic Sanctions Against South Africa, Hearings and Markup*, March 22, 23, April 20, 28, and May 3, 1988, 100th Cong., 2d sess., 1988, pp. 698–717.

11. William Howard, "Lobbying Against Apartheid," *Africa Report* 33 (March–April 1988):40.

12. "Anti-Apartheid Lobby Targets Dole, Helms," *U.S.A. Today*, March 5, 1987.

13. Prexy Nesbitt Papers, Box 2, M–92–335, 1986–1988, Chicago Committee for the Liberation of Mozambique and Angola files, State Historical Society, Madison, Wisconsin (hereafter referred to as Nesbitt Papers).

14. "Unlock Apartheid's Jails Campaign," *Africa News* 28, 2 (October 5, 1987):11.

15. American Committee on Africa, *Student Anti-Apartheid Newsletter* 2 (March 1987):1.

16. Kevin Danaher, "Confronting Southern Africa Solidarity Work," *Issue: A Journal of Opinion* 18, 2 (1990):39–43; Nesbitt Papers; *Student Anti-Apartheid Newsletter* 1 (December 1986–January 1987):4.

17. Rachel Rubin, "The Anti-Apartheid Struggle: Did It/Could It Challenge Racism in the U.S.?" *Issue: A Journal of Opinion* 24, 2 (1996):46–47.

18. John Lofland, "Consensus Movements: City Twinning and Derailed Dissent in the American Eighties," in *Research in Social Movements, Conflict and Change* 11 (Greenwich, Conn.: JAI Press, 1988), pp. 163–196.

19. New groups such as U.S. Out of Africa and Bikes for Africa illustrated the narrow objectives emerging from the organizational realm. *Encyclopedia of Associations*, Gale Research Organization, 1984–1992.

20. Jennifer Davis, James Cason, and Gail Hovey, "Economic Disengagement and South Africa: The Effectiveness and Feasibility of Implementing Sanctions and Divestment," *Law and Policy in International Business* 15 (1983):529–563; William H. Kaempfer, James A. Lehman, and Anton D. Lowenberg, "Divestment, Investment Sanctions, and Disinvestment: An Evaluation of Anti-Apartheid Policy Instruments," *International Organization* 41, 3 (Summer 1987):473.

21. David Dickson, "American Society and the African American Foreign Policy Lobby: Constraints and Opportunities," *Journal of Black Studies* 27, 2 (November 1996):139–151.

22. David M. Ricci, *The Tragedy of Political Science: Politics, Scholarship, and Democracy* (New Haven: Yale University Press, 1984), p. 300.

23. Joseph P. Nye Jr., *Bound to Lead: The Changing Nature of American Power* (New York: Basic Books, 1990).

Bibliography

Manuscript Sources

American Committee on Africa, Organizational Records. Library of the American Committee on Africa Office, New York, N.Y.

American Committee on Africa Papers. Amistad Research Center, Tulane University, New Orleans, La.

Gerald R. Ford Presidential Library, University of Michigan, Ann Arbor, Mich.

Herskovitz African Studies Research Library, Northwestern University, Evanston, Ill.

Prexy Nesbitt Papers. State Historical Society of Wisconsin, Madison, Wis.

Washington Office on Africa, Organizational Records, Washington, D.C.

Interviews

Counts, Cecilie. Interview by Connie Field, Clarity Film Productions, Berkeley, 1996.

Hecathorn, Milo Anne. Interview by Connie Field, Clarity Film Productions, Berkeley, 1995.

Herman, Jerry. Interview by Billy Nessen, Clarity Film Productions, Berkeley, 1996.

Hill, Sylvia. Interview by Connie Field, Clarity Film Productions, Berkeley, 1996.

Houser, George. Interview by Connie Field, Clarity Film Productions, Berkeley, 1996.

Robinson, Leo. Interview by Billy Nessen, Clarity Film Productions, Berkeley, 1996.

Books and Articles

Alger, Chadwick. 1990. "Grassroots Perspectives on Global Policies for Development." *Journal of Peace Research* 27 (2):155–168.

_____. 1988. *A Just Peace Through Transformation: Cultural, Economic, and Political Foundations for Change*. Boulder: Westview Press.

Arnove, Robert F., ed. 1980. *Philanthropy and Cultural Imperialism*. Bloomington: Indiana University Press.

Ball, Terence, ed. 1987. *Idioms of Inquiry: Critique and Renewal in Political Science*. Albany: State University of New York Press.

Barron, Deborah Durfee, and John Immerwahr. 1979. "The Public Views South Africa: Pathways Through a Gathering Storm." *Public Opinion* 2 (January–February):54–59.

Bender, Gerald J., James S. Coleman, and Richard S. Sklar, eds. 1986. *African Crisis Areas and U.S. Foreign Policy.* Berkeley and Los Angeles: University of California Press.

Benjamin, Medea, and Andrea Freedman. 1989. *Bridging the Global Gap: A Handbook to Linking Citizens of the First and Third Worlds.* Cabin John, Md.: Seven Locks Press.

Berman, Edward H. 1983. *The Influence of the Carnegie, Ford, and Rockefeller Foundations on American Foreign Policy.* Albany: State University of New York Press.

Boggs, Carl. 1986. *Social Movements and Political Power: Emerging Forms of Radicalism in the West.* Philadelphia: Temple University Press.

Borstelman, Thomas. 1993. *Apartheid's Reluctant Uncle: The United States and Southern Africa in the Early Cold War.* New York: Oxford University Press.

Burke, Edmund, III. 1988. *Global Crises and Social Movements: Artisans, Peasants, Populists, and the World Economy.* Boulder: Westview Press.

Chirenje, Mutero. 1987. *Ethiopianism and Afro-Americans in Southern Africa, 1883–1916.* Baton Rouge: Louisiana State University Press.

Chong, Dennis. 1991. *Collective Action and the Civil Rights Movement.* Chicago: University of Chicago Press.

Clough, Michael. 1991. *Free at Last? U.S. Policy Toward Africa and the End of the Cold War.* New York: Council on Foreign Relations.

Cohen, Joshua, and Joel Rogers. 1986. *Rules of the Game: American Politics and the Central American Movement.* Boston: South End Press.

Coker, Christopher. 1986. *The United States and South Africa, 1968–1985: Constructive Engagement and Its Critics.* Durham, N.C.: Duke University Press.

Cotter, William R., and Thomas Karis. 1976. "We Have Nothing to Hide." *Africa Report* 21 (November–December):37–45.

Culverson, Donald R. 1996. "The Politics of the Anti-Apartheid Movement in the United States, 1969–1986." *Political Science Quarterly* 111 (1) (Spring):127–149.

_____. 1989. "The USIA in Africa." *TransAfrica Forum* 6 (2) (February):60–80.

Culverson, Donald R., and Brenda Gayle Plummer. 1987. "Black Americans and Foreign Affairs: A Reassessment." *Sage Race Relations Abstracts* 12 (1) (February):21–31.

Dalton, Russell J., and Manfred Kuechler, eds. 1990. *Challenging the Political Order: New Social and Political Movements in Western Democracies.* New York: Oxford University Press.

Danaher, Kevin. 1991. *Beyond Safaris: A Guide to Building People-to-People Ties with Africa.* Trenton, N.J.: Africa World Press.

_____. 1985. *The Political Economy of U.S. Policy Toward South Africa.* Boulder: Westview Press.

Davis, Jennifer, James Cason, and Gail Hovey. 1983. "Economic Disengagement and South Africa: The Effectiveness and Feasibility of Implementing Sanctions and Divestment." *Law and Policy in International Business* 15:529–563.

de Villiers, Les. 1995. *In Sight of Surrender: The U.S. Sanctions Campaign Against South Africa, 1946–1993*. New York: Praeger.

El-Khawas, Mohamed, and Francis A. Kornegay, eds. 1975. *American-Southern African Relations: Bibliographic Essays*. Westport, Conn.: Greenwood Press.

Enloe, Cynthia. 1989. *Bananas, Beaches, and Bases: Making Feminist Sense of International Politics*. Berkeley and Los Angeles: University of California Press.

Fatton, Robert, Jr. 1986. *Black Consciousness in South Africa*. Albany: State University of New York Press.

Findlay, James F., Jr. 1993. *Church People in the Struggle: The National Council of Churches and the Black Freedom Movement*. New York: Oxford University Press.

Gaventa, John. 1980. *Power and Powerlessness: Quiescence and Rebellion in an Appalachian Valley*. Urbana: University of Illinois Press.

Gladwin, Thomas, and Ingo Walters, eds. 1980. *Multinationals Under Fire: Lessons in the Management of Conflict*. New York: John Wiley and Sons.

Hamilton, John Maxwell. 1990. *Entangling Alliances: How the Third World Shapes Our Lives*. Cabin John, Md.: Seven Locks Press.

Harvey, David. 1989. *The Condition of Postmodernity: An Enquiry into the Origins of Cultural Change*. Cambridge, Mass.: Basil Blackwell.

Hauck, David, Meg Voorhes, and Glenn Goldberg. 1983. *Two Decades of Debate: The Controversy over U.S. Companies in South Africa*. Washington, D.C.: Investor Responsibility Research Center.

Hero, Alfred O., and John Barratt, eds. 1981. *The American People and South Africa: Publics, Elites, and Policymaking Processes*. Lexington, Mass.: Lexington Books.

Hirsch, Eric L. 1990. "Sacrifice for the Cause: Group Processes, Recruitment, and Commitment in a Student Social Movement." *American Sociological Review* 55 (April):243–254.

Houser, George. 1989. *No One Can Stop the Rain: Glimpses of Africa's Liberation Struggle*. New York: Pilgrim Press.

_____. 1976. "Meeting Africa's Challenge: The Story of the American Committee on Africa." *Issue: A Quarterly Journal of Africanist Opinion* 6 (2–3) (Summer–Fall):16–26.

Hull, Richard W. 1990. *American Enterprise in South Africa: Historical Dimensions of Engagement and Disengagement*. New York: New York University Press.

Jackson, Henry F. 1982. *From the Congo to Soweto: U.S. Foreign Policy Toward Africa Since 1960*. New York: William Morrow.

Jenkins, J. Craig. 1985. *The Politics of Insurgency: The Farm Worker Movement in the 1960s*. New York: Columbia University Press.

Kann, Mark E. 1986. *Middle-Class Radicalism in Santa Monica*. Philadelphia: Temple University Press.

Kariel, Henry. 1989. "Praxis: The Repressed Potential of Political Science." *Polity* 21 (2):401–408.

Keto, Clement T. "American Involvement in South Africa, 1870–1915: The Role of Americans in the Creation of Modern South Africa." Ph.D. diss., Georgetown University, 1972.

Klandermans, Bert. 1991. "The Peace Movement and Social Movement Theory." *International Social Movement Research*, vol. 3, pp. 1–39. Greenwich, Conn.: JAI Press.

Lake, Anthony. 1976. *The "Tar Baby" Option: American Policy Toward Southern Rhodesia*. New York: Columbia University Press.

Leape, Jonathan, Bo Baskin, and S. Underhill. 1984. *Business in the Shadow of Apartheid: A Survey of U.S. Companies*. Lexington, Mass.: Lexington.

Lodge, Tom. 1983. *Black Politics in South Africa Since 1945*. New York: Longman.

Lofland, John. 1989. "Consensus Movements: City Twinning and Derailed Dissent in the American Eighties." *Research in Social Movements, Conflict, and Change* 11:163–196.

Love, Janice. 1985. *The U.S. Anti-Apartheid Movement: Local Activism in Global Politics*. New York: Praeger.

Luke, Timothy W. 1989. *Screens of Power: Ideology, Domination, and Resistance in Informational Society*. Urbana and Chicago: University of Illinois Press.

Martin, Patrick Henry. "American Views on South Africa, 1948–1972." Ph.D. diss., Louisiana State University, 1974.

McAdam, Doug. 1982. *Political Process and the Development of Black Insurgency, 1930–1970*. Chicago: University of Chicago Press.

McCann, Michael. 1986. *Taking Reform Seriously: Perspectives on Public Interest Liberalism*. Ithaca: Cornell University Press.

McCaughey, Robert. 1984. *International Studies and Academic Enterprise: A Chapter in the Enclosure of American Learning*. New York: Columbia University Press.

McCrea, Frances, and Gerald Markle. 1989. "Atomic Scientists and Protests." *Research in Social Movements, Conflict, and Change* 11:219–233.

Metz, Steven. 1986. "The Anti-Apartheid Movement and the Populist Instinct in American Politics." *Political Science Quarterly* 101 (3) (Fall):379–395.

Meyer, David. 1990. *A Winter of Nuclear Discontent: The Nuclear Freeze and American Politics*. New York: Praeger.

Minter, William. 1986. *King Solomon's Mines Revisited: Western Interests and the Burdened History of Southern Africa*. New York: Basic Books.

Morris, Aldon D., and Carol McClurg Mueller, eds. 1992. *Frontiers in Social Movement Theory*. New Haven: Yale University Press.

Morris, Aldon D., and Cedric Herring. 1987. "Theory and Research in Social Movements: A Critical Review." In Samuel Long, ed., *Annual Review of Political Science*, vol. 2, pp. 137–198. Norwood, N.J.: Ablex.

Myers, Desaix, III, with Kenneth Propp, David Hauck, and David M. Liff. 1980. *U.S. Business in South Africa: The Economic, Political, and Moral Issues*. Bloomington: Indiana University Press.

Nixon, Rob. 1994. *Homelands, Harlem, and Hollywood: South African Culture and the World Beyond*. New York: Routledge.

Noer, Thomas J. 1985. *Cold War and Black Liberation: The United States and White Rule in Africa, 1948–1969*. Columbia: University of Missouri Press.

_____. 1978. *Briton, Boer, and Yankee: The United States and South Africa, 1870–1914*. Kent, Ohio: Kent State University Press.

Offe, Claus. 1985a. *Disorganized Capitalism: Contemporary Transformations of Work and Politics*. Cambridge, Mass.: MIT Press.

_____. 1985b. "New Social Movements: Challenging the Boundaries of Institutional Politics." *Social Forces* 52 (4) (Winter):818–820.

Ogene, F. Chidozie. 1983. *Interest Groups and the Shaping of Foreign Policy: Four Case Studies of United States Foreign Policy*. New York: St. Martin's Press.

Oliver, Pamela E. 1989. "Bringing the Crowd Back In: The Nonorganizational Elements of Social Movements." *Research in Social Movements, Conflict, and Change* 11:1–30.

Pallister, David, Sarah Stewart, and Ian Lepper. 1988. *South Africa, Inc.: The Oppenheimer Empire*. New Haven: Yale University Press.

Posel, Deborah. 1991. *The Making of Apartheid, 1948–1961: Conflict and Compromise*. New York: Clarendon Press.

Price, Robert M. 1991. *The Apartheid State in Crisis: Political Transformation in South Africa, 1975–1990*. New York: Oxford University Press.

Robinson, Pearl T., and Elliott P. Skinner, eds. 1983. *Transformation and Resiliency in Africa: As Seen by Afro-American Scholars*. Washington, D.C.: Howard University Press.

Rogers, Barbara. 1976. *White Wealth and Black Poverty*. Westport, Conn.: Greenwood Press.

Rosenthal, Eric. 1968. *Stars and Stripes in Africa*. Johannesburg: G. Routledge and Sons.

Salisbury, Robert H. 1989. "Political Movements in American Politics: An Essay on Concept and Analysis." *National Political Science Review* 1:15–30.

Schiller, Herbert. 1984. *Information and the Crisis Economy*. Norwood, N.J.: Ablex.

Schraeder, Peter J. 1994. *United States Foreign Policy Toward Africa: Incrementalism, Crisis, and Change*. New York: Cambridge University Press.

Seidman, Ann. 1990. *Apartheid, Militarism, and the U.S. Southeast*. Trenton, N.J.: Africa World Press.

_____. 1985. *The Roots of Crisis in Southern Africa*. Trenton, N.J.: Africa World Press.

Shepherd, George. 1977. *Anti-Apartheid: Transnational Conflict and Western Policy in the Liberation of South Africa*. Westport, Conn.: Greenwood Press.

Staniland, Martin. 1991. *American Intellectuals and African Nationalists, 1955–1970*. New Haven: Yale University Press.

_____. 1983–1984. "Africa, the American Intelligentsia, and the Shadow of Vietnam." *Political Science Quarterly* 98 (4) (Winter):595–616.

_____. 1983. "Who Needs African Studies?" *African Studies Review* 26 (3–4) (September–December):77–97.

Study Commission on U.S. Policy Toward Southern Africa. 1986. *South Africa: Time Running Out*. 2d ed. Berkeley and Los Angeles: University of California Press.

Tarrow, Sidney. 1983. *Struggling to Reform: Social Movements and Policy Change During Cycles of Protest*. Ithaca: Cornell Studies in International Affairs.

Tolley, Howard. 1990–1991. "Interest Group Litigation to Enforce Human Rights." *Political Science Quarterly* 105 (4) (Winter):617–638.

Vellela, Tony. 1988. *New Voices: Student Political Activism in the '80s and '90s*. Boston: South End Press.

Walker, R.B.J. 1988. *One World, Many Worlds: Struggles for a Just World Peace*. Boulder: Lynne Rienner.

Walker, R.B.J., and Saul H. Mendlovitz, eds. 1990. *Contending Sovereignties: Redefining Political Community*. Boulder: Lynne Rienner.

Weissbrodt, David, and Georghina Mahoney. 1986. "International Legal Action Against Apartheid." *Law and Inequality* October:485–508.

West, Guida, and Rhoda Lois Blumberg, eds. 1990. *Women and Social Protest*. New York: Oxford University Press.

Index